yourself

german starter kit
coursebook
elisabeth smith

The publisher has used its best endeavours to ensure that the URLs for external websites referred to in this book are correct and active at the time of going to press. However, the publisher and the author have no responsibility for the websites and can make no guarantee that a site will remain live or that the content will remain relevant, decent or appropriate.

For UK order enquiries: please contact Bookpoint Ltd, 130 Milton Park, Abingdon, Oxon, OX14 4SB. Telephone: +44 (0) 1235 827720. Fax: +44 (0) 1235 400454. Lines are open 09.00–17.00, Monday to Saturday, with a 24-hour message answering service. Details about our titles and how to order are available at www.teachyourself.co.uk

For USA order enquiries: please contact McGraw-Hill Customer Services, PO Box 545, Blacklick, OH 43004-0545, USA. Telephone: 1-800-722-4726. Fax: 1-614-755-5645.

For Canada order enquiries: please contact McGraw-Hill Ryerson Ltd, 300 Water St, Whitby, Ontario, L1N 9B6, Canada. Telephone: 905 430 5000. Fax: 905 430 5020.

Long renowned as the authoritative source for self-guided learning – with more than 50 million copies sold worldwide – the **teach yourself** series includes over 500 titles in the fields of languages, crafts, hobbies, business, computing and education.

British Library Cataloguing in Publication Data: a catalogue record for this title is available from the British Library.

Library of Congress Catalog Card Number: on file.

First published in UK 2007 by Hodder Education, 338 Euston Road, London, NW1 3BH.

First published in US 2007 by The McGraw-Hill Companies, Inc.

This edition published 2007.

The **teach yourself** name is a registered trade mark of Hodder Headline.

Typeset by Transet Limited, Coventry, England.
Printed in China for Hodder Education, a division of Hodder Headline, 338 Euston Road, London, NW1 3BH.

Impression number   10 9 8 7 6 5 4 3 2 1
Year   2010 2009 2008 2007

contents

Read this first – and meet your personal tutor!

Teaching yourself a foreign language can be quite difficult, because:

- There's no one to talk to
- There's no one to correct you
- There's no one to tell you if you are doing well

That's why the **Teach Yourself German Starter Kit** comes with a built-in **personal tutor**. So you are never left on your own or tempted to give up.

With your **tutor** at your side you'll work through your daily programme of listening, learning, speaking, and more speaking, until you get it right. But it's all quick and easy.

There are hardly any written exercises in this book. After all, you want to *speak* German, not hand over pieces of paper, to find out where the shops are.

At the end of each week your **tutor** will check your speaking progress. You'll be amazed at the result!

On Day 1 you'll meet Paul and Claire. They are fed up with the bad weather and are off to Germany. They do the things most people do – shopping, eating out, sightseeing, even looking at cars and going to the doctor's.

As they speak German to each other all the time (aren't they clever!), you'll pick up all the important words which *you* will want to use. That's how easy it is.

There's only one thing you must do: follow the daily programme as suggested. When you have had a look at the short dialogue and the box of **New words** go straight to **'What to do today'** and work your way down. Don't skip bits. Everything is there for a purpose: to get you to speak fluently – fast!

Now read the next page, and then you are ready to begin.

Start with the first **CD** and meet your **tutor**!

CD1

Introduction: Track 1
Week 1: Tracks 2–8
Week 2: Tracks 9–15
Week 3: Tracks 16–20

CD2

Week 3: Tracks 1–2
Week 4: Tracks 3–9
Week 5: Tracks 10–16
Week 6: Tracks 17–23
Week 7: Tracks 24–30

Recorded at Alchemy Studios, London. Cast: Walter Bohnacker, Stephan Erdman, Sylvia Hensel, Andy Johnson, Ruth Rach.

why this starter kit works

With this **Starter Kit** anyone can learn German in just 7 weeks. Because …

✓ There are only **210 German words** in the whole coursebook. That's enough for basic communication.

✓ You learn **five new words a day**. That's manageable. Anyone can learn **five** words in a day!

✓ You have **Flash cards** to help you. They make learning less boring as you 'turn and learn' and reshuffle the pack.

✓ You start speaking in **whole sentences** from Day 1. That's what you want.

✓ There's no complicated grammar, just a few **Nuts and bolts**. They'll help you put things together.

✓ You'll learn to say things by heart. That's most important. It will make you **speak fluently – fast**. So talk to the dog, to the fridge or to the unsuspecting offspring – OUT LOUD! This will speed up the sentence's journey from your brain to your mouth.

And best of all …

✓ There's your **personal tutor** on the two **CD**s, guiding, explaining, motivating and testing, and making sure you'll do well on the **Progress chart**.

There's also some 'First Aid' in the **Kit**, a booklet with lots of additional and useful information on **shopping**, **eating out** and **travelling**, even some **medical advice** plus a **mini-dictionary** of all your **new words**. This is your **Traveller's companion**, for you to keep in your bag or your pocket when you are off to Germany, Austria or Switzerland.

Finally, when you have finished the course, filled in your **Certificate** and are back from your trip, I'd love to hear from you. You can write to me c/o Hodder Education or e-mail me at **www.ellisabeth-smith.co.uk**

Good luck, and ... Auf Wiedersehen!

progress chart

This is where you record your weekly result and watch your progress.

Each week write your score in one of the boxes. If your score is less than 60% – highly unlikely! – spend an extra day going over the **New words** and the exercises of that week. Then take the Day 7 test again.

	60–70%	70–80%	80–90%	90–100%
Week 1				
Week 2				
Week 3				
Week 4				
Week 5				
Week 6				
Week 7				

At the end of the course throw out your worst score. (We all have a bad week at times.) Then add up the remaining six scores. Divide the total by 6 to get your average score.

Total of six scores _____ **divided by 6**

= my final score [   ] %

Match up your final score with one of these:

60–70% = good   70–80% = very good
80–90% = excellent   90%+ = outstanding

You are now ready to write your course result on your **Certificate** on page 116.

Congratulations!

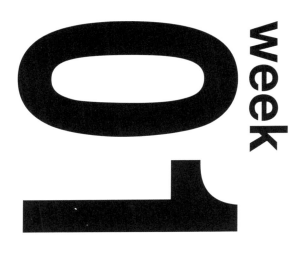

week 01

wir gehen Ski fahren

we are going skiing

The story …

A Sunday evening in February. It is cold and dark. It is raining. Paul and Claire are fed up. Then Paul has a brillliant idea …!

Day 1

What to do today

✓ Listen to **Welcome to the German starter kit** on the first **recording**
✓ Listen to today's **Story** and the **New words**
✓ Listen again, until you can say all the words correctly
✓ Listen to **How to say German words**
✓ Learn today's five **New words** in the box, the ones on the left-hand side, using the **Flash cards** in the **Kit**
✓ Read through the **Nuts and bolts** and listen to the **recording**
✓ Learn the **Story** by heart and say it OUT LOUD

The story

Paul   **Wir gehen Ski fahren!**
Claire **Toll! Berge, Schnee, Glühwein …**
Paul   **Wir fliegen nach München – im Februar.**

Today's new words		Tomorrow's new words	
wir gehen	*we go*	Glühwein	*mulled wine (hot wine with sugar and spices)*
Ski fahren	*to ski, skiing*		
toll	*great*		
die Berge	*the mountains*	wir fliegen	*we fly*
der Schnee	*the snow*	nach	*to*
		München	*Munich*
		im Februar	*in February*

Day 2

What to do today

✓ Listen to **How to say German words**
✓ Listen to the **recording – Story** and **New words**
✓ Listen to the **New sentences**
✓ Learn today's five **New words** in the box, the ones on the right-hand side, using the **Flash cards**
✓ Learn the **New sentences** by heart and say them OUT LOUD
✓ **Let's speak German!** Do the exercise below and say the sentences OUT LOUD. Then check them on the **recording**

Yesterday's new words		Today's new words	
wir gehen	*we go*	Glühwein	*mulled wine*
Ski fahren	*to ski, skiing*		*(hot wine with*
toll	*great*		*sugar and spices)*
die Berge	*the mountains*	wir fliegen	*we fly*
der Schnee	*the snow*	nach	*to*
		München	*Munich*
		im Februar	*in February*

Today's new sentences

Wir fliegen nach Amerika – im Februar. Wir gehen nach Berlin – im April. Ski fahren? Toll!

Let's speak German!

Say these sentences in German. Speak OUT LOUD!

- We fly to Frankfurt.
- We go to Munich.
- We go in February.
- The snow is (ist) great.
- We go skiing in April.

Day 3

What to do today

✓ Listen to the **Story** and **New words**. Listen again until you can say all the words correctly
✓ Learn the **New words** in the box. Use the **Flash cards**
✓ Listen to the **New sentences**
✓ Learn the **New sentences** by heart and say them OUT LOUD
✓ **Nuts** and **bolts**: Listen to the **recording**, then read and … learn them
✓ **Let's speak German!** Do the exercise below and say the sentences OUT LOUD. Then check them on the **recording**

The story
Claire   Aber wir haben nicht viel Geld.

Today's new words

aber	*but*
wir haben	*we have*
nicht	*not, don't*
viel	*much, a lot of*
das Geld	*the money*

Today's new sentences
Glühwein? Toll! Wir haben viel Geld. Aber wir haben nicht viel Schnee im Februar.

Nuts and bolts

nicht

To say *not* or *don't* you simply use **nicht**.

The snow is *not* great.   Der Schnee ist **nicht** toll.
We *don't* have a lot of money.   Wir haben **nicht** viel Geld.

Let's speak German!

Say these sentences in German – OUT LOUD!

- We are not flying to Bonn.
- We are not going to Düsseldorf.
- Skiing in England is not great.
- We don't have a lot of snow in London.
- Hamburg is not great in November.

Day 4

What to do today

✓ Listen to the **Story** and the **New words**. Listen again until you can say all the words correctly
✓ Listen to the **New sentences**
✓ Listen to **How to say German words**
✓ **Nuts and bolts**: Listen to the **recording**, then read and … learn them
✓ Learn the five **New words** in the box. Use the **Flash cards** to make it easy
✓ Learn the **New sentences** by heart and say them OUT LOUD
✓ **Let's speak German!** Say the sentences below OUT LOUD and then check them on the **recording**

The story

Paul   Ah! Ich habe einen Freund, Helmut Schmidt. Er hat ein Haus in München.
Claire   Ein Haus in München? Toll!

Today's new words

ich habe	*I have*
ein, eine, einen	*a*
der Freund, die Freundin	*the male friend, the female friend*
er hat	*he has*
das Haus	*the house*

Today's new sentences

Ich habe ein Haus in London aber nicht viel Geld. Paul hat einen Freund in München. Claire hat eine Freundin in Berlin.

Nuts and bolts

Did you notice?
der Freund, **die** Freundin, **das** Haus, **die** Berge
der, **die**, **das** – and sometimes even **dem** or **den** – all mean *the*.

So how do you know which one to use? Here's the good news: Try to learn each word correctly – **der** Schnee, **die** Freundin, **das** Geld. With more than one item – the mountain**s** – **die** Berge – always use **die**.

But if you muddle things up it's not a big problem. People will still understand you perfectly.

ein, and **eine** – and sometimes **einem**, **einer** or **einen** – all mean *a*.

Try to learn the words as you meet them: Ich habe **ein** Haus. Paul hat **einen** Freund. But don't worry if you mix them up.

Let's speak German!

Say these sentences in German. Speak out loud!

- I have a girlfriend, Brigitte.
- We have a house in Lübeck.
- Gerhard has money, but not a lot.
- He does not have much wine in the house.
- The mountain does not have a lot of snow.
- We don't fly to Munich in November.
- We are going skiing in Innsbruck.
- The house is great in the snow.

Day 5

What to do today

✓ Listen to the **Story** and then the **New words**
✓ Listen to the **New sentences**
✓ Listen to **How to say German words**
✓ **Nuts and bolts**: Listen to the **recording**, then read and … learn them
✓ Learn the **New words** with the **Flash cards**
✓ Learn the **New sentences** by heart and say them OUT LOUD
✓ **Let's speak German!** Complete the sentences below. Say them OUT LOUD, then check them on the **recording**

The story

Claire	Aber wie fliegen wir? Birmingham nach München ist teuer.
Paul	Ja, fliegen ist teuer.
Claire	Haben wir nicht einen Freund bei Lufthansa?

Today's new words

wie?	*how?*
ist	*is*
teuer	*expensive*
ja	*yes*
bei	*at*

Today's new sentences

Wie teuer ist London? Teuer? Ja, viel Geld! München ist nicht teuer – bei Helmut, Pauls Freund.

Nuts and bolts

Asking questions

This is very easy in German. You simply reverse the word order:

London ist teuer. London is expensive. **Ist London teuer?** *Is* London expensive?

Wir haben Geld. We have money. **Haben wir Geld?** Do we have money? (*Have* we money?)

Let's speak German!

1 Put the right word in the gap and say the sentences OUT LOUD.

- Wir _____ einen Freund in Berlin.
- _____ teuer ist London?
- Ich _____ ein tolles Haus.
- Ilse _____ viel _____.
- Wir _____ im Februar Ski _____.

2 Now tell me in German that you have

- a female friend
- a house in Bremen
- not a lot of money
- a male friend in Düsseldorf

3 Now turn these statements into questions

- Wir haben einen Freund bei Lufthansa.
- Helmut hat nicht viel Geld.
- Pauls Haus ist toll.
- Wir fahren im April nach Heidelberg.

Day 6

What to do today
✓ Listen to the **Story** and the **New words**
✓ Learn the **New words**, using the **Flash cards**. You now know your first 30 German words (and a few extras)!
✓ Learn the **New sentences** by heart and say them OUT LOUD
✓ **Nuts and bolts**: Listen to the **recording**, then read and … learn them
✓ **Let's speak German!** Say the sentences below OUT LOUD and then check them on the **recording**

The story
Paul **Wir haben ein Auto. Wir nehmen das Auto. Das ist nicht teuer.**
Claire **Ja, das ist billig. Aber … das Auto ist kaputt.**

Today's new words
das Auto	*the car*
wir nehmen	*we take*
das	*the, that*
billig	*cheap*
kaputt	*broken, out of order*

Today's new sentences
Claires Freundin Helga hat ein Auto. Wie ist das Auto? Das Auto ist toll aber teuer. Helmuts Auto ist billig aber kaputt. Wir nehmen Helgas Auto.

Nuts and bolts

Doing things (or verbs)
German verbs are quite easy. Nearly all of them end in **-en**. So far you have learnt **gehen**, **fahren**, **nehmen** and **haben**. To say *we go* or *we have* it's simply **wir gehen** or **wir haben**. But if you want to say *I go* or *I take* you have to drop the **n**. So it's **ich gehe** and **ich nehme**.

When you talk about someone or something else you drop the **-en** and usually just replace it with a **-t**. So *he goes* or *Helmut goes* becomes **er geht** or **Helmut geht**.

Sometimes the word or a letter in the word changes altogether. That's why *he has* becomes **er hat**.

If you wanted to say *he takes* it becomes **er nimmt** (**not** er nehmt). Or if you wanted to say *she goes* (by car) it's **sie fährt** (note the dots!). But that is for another day.

Let's speak German!

Say these sentences in German. Speak out loud!

- The wine is not cheap.
- The house is expensive.
- Uwe's car is cheap.
- Does he have a girlfriend?
- We take the car to Freiburg.
- How do we take the car?
- That is Elke's boyfriend.
- That is cheap but broken.

Day 7

What to do today

Today you are going to do a lot of talking. First, listen to the whole **Story**, then read it – OUT LOUD. Then do the two practice rounds below and, finally, test yourself. You'll be surprised how much you can say in German already, after only ONE week!

Here's this week's whole story …

Paul	**Wir gehen Ski fahren!**
Claire	**Toll! Berge, Schnee, Glühwein …**
Paul	**Wir fliegen nach München – im Februar.**
Claire	**Aber wir haben nicht viel Geld.**
Paul	**Ah! Ich habe einen Freund, Helmut Schmidt. Er hat ein Haus in München.**
Claire	**Ein Haus in München? Toll! Aber wie fliegen wir? Birmingham nach München ist teuer.**
Paul	**Ja, fliegen ist teuer.**
Claire	**Haben wir nicht einen Freund bei Lufthansa?**
Paul	**Wir haben ein Auto. Wir nehmen das Auto. Das ist nicht teuer.**
Claire	**Ja, das ist billig. Aber … das Auto ist kaputt.**

Tell me, tell me (in German!) that …

- … you (and your friend) are going to Zurich. (**Wir fliegen** …)
- … you are going by plane, you are not taking the car, the car has broken down.
- … you have a friend, Erika, in St Moritz … Erika has a house.
- … St Moritz is great. St Moritz has a lot of snow and mountains … the mulled wine is cheap. You are not going to take much money with you (with you = **mit dir**) … but you are going to ski a lot.

When you have said it all OUT LOUD, listen to the **recording** and check it.

Tell me more …

Answer these questions, starting with **ja** *yes* and then again with **nein** *no*.

Here's an example:

> *Question*: Ist das Hotel billig?
> *Answer*: Ja, das Hotel ist billig. Nein, das Hotel ist nicht billig.

Now over to you:

- Haben wir viel Geld im Haus?
- Wie ist Innsbruck, teuer?
- Nehmen wir das kaputte Auto?
- Haben wir viele Freunde in Deutschland?
- Haben die Berge viel Schnee bei Salzburg?

When you have said it all OUT LOUD listen to the **recording** and check if your answers were right. If you got into a muddle just do it again.

In a flash

Now take out the five **Flash sentences** and with the English facing you, say the German – in a flash! Then turn the card over and check.

Testing, testing

Close the book and listen one more time to the whole story of Day 7. Then, without looking at the **Flash cards** – write down all the German words you can remember. Score 50% for remembering 15 words and then 5% for each additional word. If you remember 25 words or more you'll score 100%.

Your result this week

Write your score for the week here:

My score _____ %   **Date** _____

Now mark up your **Progress chart** on page ix.

Finally …

German people will really appreciate your making an effort to speak their language and are full of praise when you try. They won't mind at all if you make mistakes. German spoken with an English accent sounds very attractive!

week

02

wo ist Elke?

where is Elke?

The story continues …

On arrival at Munich airport Paul and Claire fight their way through the crowds. They are looking for Elke, Helmut's girlfriend, whom they have not met before.

Day 1

What to do today

✓ Read today's five **New words**
✓ Read and work out the **Story**, and the **New sentences**
✓ Listen to the **New words**, the **Story** and the **New sentences** on the **recording**
✓ **Nuts and bolts:** Listen to the **recording**, then read and … learn them
✓ Learn today's five **New words** and the five **New sentences** by heart
✓ Say the **New sentences** OUT LOUD
✓ Test yourself with **Let's speak German!**, then check your answers with the **recording**

The story

Paul	Wo ist Elke?
Claire	Elke ist nicht hier. Aber viele Leute.
Paul	Das gefällt mir nicht. Wir nehmen den Bus.

Today's new words

wo	*where*
hier	*here*
viele Leute	*many people*
das gefällt mir nicht	*I don't like that*
der, dem, den Bus	*the bus*

Today's new sentences

Der Bus gefällt mir nicht. Wo ist das Auto? Aber der Bus ist hier. Viele Leute nehmen den Bus. Der Bus ist billig.

Nuts and bolts

der, dem, den

Hier ist **der** Bus.   *Here is the bus.*
Ich fahre mit **dem** Bus.   *I go by/with the bus.*
Ich nehme **den** Bus.   *I take the bus.*

In English it's just THE BUS. In German it can be **der**, **dem** or **den** Bus depending on the word that precedes the bus or its position in the sentence.

No need to feel suicidal!

Rather than trying to learn lots of complicated rules just try to remember some of the short sample sentences above. And if you pick the wrong one? No problem. Nobody will fall about laughing.

I like that – I don't like that
In German we say **das gefällt mir – das gefällt mir nicht**. I like to think of it as 'that pleases me – that pleases me not'. So when you want to say that you like Paul's new Porsche think 'Paul's Porsche pleases me'. **Pauls Porsche gefällt mir**. 'I don't like the snow'. **Der Schnee gefällt mir nicht**.

Let's speak German!

1 Say these sentences in German OUT LOUD and practise *like* and *don't like*.

- I like skiing.
- I don't like that.
- Do I like the car?
- Yes, I like the car.
- Do I like the bus?
- No, I don't like the bus

2 Complete these sentences. Then give two answers in German, starting with **ja** and **nein**.

- Gefällt _____ das Haus?
- Nehmen wir _____ Bus?
- Fliegen _____ Leute nach Berlin?
- _____ ist das Auto? Hier in Frankfurt?
- Haben _____ viel Geld im Hotel?

Day 2

What to do today
✓ Read today's five **New words**
✓ Read and work out the **Story** and the **New sentences** and listen to it all on the **recording**
✓ Learn today's five **New words** and the **New sentences** by heart
✓ Speak to me! Do the three lots of **Let's speak German!**
✓ Check your progress with the **recording**

The story
Paul Einen Moment, Elke ist vielleicht hier rechts.
Claire Nein, sie ist nicht hier. Nehmen wir ein Taxi?
Paul Nein, wir nehmen den Bus.
Entschuldigen Sie, wo ist der Bus hier nach München?

Today's new words
einen Moment	*a moment*
sie	*she*
vielleicht	*perhaps*
rechts	*right, on the right*
entschuldigen Sie	*excuse me*

Today's new sentences
Der Bus ist nicht hier. Entschuldigen Sie, ist ein Taxi nach Berlin teuer? Ja? Wir nehmen vielleicht ein Auto. Einen Moment, hier rechts ist der Bus!

Let's speak German!
1 Answer in German, in full sentences using the word/s in brackets.

• Wie ist der Bus nach Hamburg? (billig)
• Wo ist das Auto für meine Freundin? (hier rechts)
• Haben Sie einen Moment, bitte? (ja)
• Ist sie vielleicht bei Helmut? (nein)
• Hat Elke vielleicht einen Freund? (ja)

2 Now say these sentences in German, starting with **entschuldigen Sie**.

- Excuse me, do a lot of people take the bus?
- Excuse me, but I don't like the car.
- Excuse me, but we don't have a lot of money.
- Excuse me, but I don't like the snow.
- Excuse me, where is she?
- Excuse me, but that car has had it.

3 Put the right form of **haben** into these sentences.

- Ich _____ viele Leute im Haus.
- Helmut _____ ein kaputtes Auto.
- Die Leute in London _____ viel Geld.
- Wir _____ hier vielleicht Schnee im April.
- Natascha _____ eine tolle Freundin.
- Die Freundin _____ ein Haus in Amerika.
- Ich _____ viel Glühwein im Hotel.

Day 3

What to do today

✓ Read today's five **New words**
✓ Read and work out today's **Story** with the **New words**. Listen to it all on the **recording**
✓ **Nuts and bolts:** Listen to the **recording**, then read and … learn them
✓ Learn today's five **New words**. Then listen to the **New sentences** and learn them by heart
✓ **Let's speak German!** It's your speaking practice – so speak OUT LOUD!
✓ Check your progress with the **recording**

The story

Elke	**Der Bus nach München ist hier links. Aber … sind Sie nicht Paul? Ich bin Elke!**
Paul	**Hallo Elke, ja ich bin Paul. Und hier ist Claire.**

Today's new words

links	*left, on the left*
Sie sind, sind Sie?	*you are, are you? they are, are they?*
hallo	*hello*
ich bin	*I am*
und	*and*

Today's new sentences

Hallo, ich bin … (*give your name*). Und Sie sind … ?
Entschuldigen Sie, wo ist hier ein Taxi? Hier links?

Nuts and bolts

It's back to the tool kit and your first action word or verb: **to be** or **… not to be**.

I like to think of verbs as the skeleton of the language. Without bones you simply fall down. And you certainly can't walk about in Germany and make sentences without verbs.

The good news is that there are only 12 essential verbs in this **Kit**. These 12 verbs you'll have to learn otherwise you'll come unstuck. But they aren't difficult and are quite similar to English.

And there's a bit of extra good news: I have cut down every verb to the minimum. So unlike a proper school book you are getting the **Starter Kit's** special condensed version of each verb. That means you save 33% studying time – quite a large discount!

You already know how to say in German: *I am*, *you are* and *she is*. Now take a quick look at **to be – sein** in the **Essential verbs** in the **Traveller's companion** on page 20 and fill in the gaps so you can say *he is*, *it is*, *we are* and *they are*.

Easy? Easy!

You: Du or Sie?

There is a choice of saying *you* in German when addressing someone: the formal **Sie** and the informal **Du**.

Germans usually use **Sie** when they talk to each other. **Du** is only used in the family, among children and young adults, and between best friends. Even people who have known each other for years usually address each other with **Sie** and the surname. When you are in Germany use **Sie**. It's also easier.

Let's speak German!

1 Say these sentences in German:

- She is Heidi Müller.
- We are in (on) the bus in Berlin.
- He is in Manchester in August.
- Karin and Ilse are in Dortmund.
- I am Klaus Becker.
- It is perhaps broken.
- Is that the car?
- Are you here at the (beim) Oktoberfest?
- How are the people in the hotel?
- The taxi is here, on the left.
- Cars are not cheap in England.

2 Now put the right words into the gaps and then say each sentence out loud.

Use all these words:

> **mir   haben   einen   Sie   sind   wo**

- Die Leute hier _____ nicht viel Geld.
- Sind _____ vielleicht Herr Schumacher?
- Und _____ ist das billige Auto?
- Die Bar gefällt _____, aber wo ist der Wein?
- Hier links _____ die Berge.
- Entschuldigen Sie, _____ Moment, ich bin im Auto.

Day 4

What to do today

✓ Read today's five **New words**
✓ Read and work out the **Story**, and the **New words**
✓ Listen to it all on the **recording**
✓ Read the **Nuts and bolts**
✓ Look at the **Traveller's companion**. On page 17 you'll find the **names of the months**. Listen to the **recording** and read along OUT LOUD
✓ Learn today's five **New words**. Then listen to, and learn the **New sentences** by heart
✓ Speaking practice – always OUT LOUD: say the **New sentences** and then do the exercise in **Let's speak German!**
✓ Listen to the **Speaking practice** on the **recording**

The story

Elke   **Hallo Claire. Wie geht's? Gut? Es tut mir leid, aber ich habe kein Auto. Das Auto ist kaputt. Wir nehmen den Bus ... in zwei Stunden.**

Today's new words

Wie geht's?	*How are you? How is it going?*
gut	*good*
Es tut mir leid.	*I am sorry.*
kein/keine, kein Auto	*no, no car*
in zwei Stunden	*in two hours*

Today's new sentences

Der Airport Bus ist kaputt, und wir fliegen nach Köln in zwei Stunden! Wie geht's Helmut? Nicht gut? Es tut mir leid!

Nuts and Bolts

Brace yourself.

You are about to get a first taste of the unusual German word order. Here's a harmless looking sentence:

We are going in April to Berlin. **Wir fahren im April nach Berlin.**

But if you said … *In April we are going to Berlin*, the action word **fahren** would rush forward, past the word **wir** and you would say … Im April **fahren wir** nach Berlin.

This happens every time a sentence starts with an 'introduction', something that is not the main subject of the sentence. Here's another example:

I take the car. **Ich nehme das Auto.** *Perhaps I take the car.* **Vielleicht nehme ich das Auto.**

And if you forget and say: **Vielleicht ich nehme das Auto**? Nobody will have a heart attack. Everyone will understand you.

Let's speak German!

Here are 12 destinations – one for every month: Hamburg, Hannover, Köln, Dresden, Leipzig, Berlin, München, Nürnberg, Frankfurt, Düsseldorf, Dortmund and Stuttgart. When you know the names of the 12 months join months and destinations like this:

Im Januar fahre ich nach Hamburg. Im Februar fahre ich…

Day 5

What to do today

✓ Read today's five **New words**
✓ Read and work out the **Story** and the **New sentences**. Listen to it all on the **recording**
✓ **Nuts and bolts**. Read about **möchten** and a shortcut
✓ Look at the **Traveller's companion:** Check out the essential verb **möchten** on page 23
✓ Learn today's five **New words** and the **New sentences** by heart
✓ Say the **New sentences** OUT LOUD
✓ **Let's speak German!** Do the exercise and practise **möchten**
✓ Check your speaking practice with the **recording**

The story

Claire	**In zwei Stunden? Wo ist ein Café oder eine Bar? Ich möchte einen Schnaps.**
Paul	**Einen Schnaps? Nein! Zwei Cappuccino, bitte. Und Sie, Elke? Möchten Sie einen Cappuccino?**
Elke	**Ja, bitte, und vielleicht ... einen Glühwein ...**

Today's new words

oder	*or*
ich möchte	*I would like*
Schnaps	*schnapps, a type of spirit*
möchten Sie?	*would you like?*
bitte	*please*

Today's new sentences

Möchten Sie das Auto? Nein, das Auto gefällt mir nicht. Ich möchte nach Hamburg. Wo ist hier ein Bus oder ein Taxi, bitte?

Nuts and bolts

möchten
Did you notice? It's er, sie, es möcht**e**. No **-t** at the end.

shortcut
Helmut möchte nach Hamburg. *Helmut would like (to go) to Hamburg.*

In every day German the *go* or *to go* is usually dropped if you *would like* to go, *want* to go or *must* go somewhere. It's kind of taken for granted that you intend to *go*.

> *We would like to go to Florida in February.* **Wir möchten im Februar nach Florida.** (Me, too!)

Let's speak German!

Say in German:

- Would you like a schnapps?
- No, I would not like a schnapps, I would like a Coca Cola, please.
- I am sorry, we have no Coca Cola.
- And I have no money.
- In May Karin would like to go to England.
- She would like to go to London.
- I am sorry, I don't like that.
- She has no money, and she has no car.

Day 6

What to do today

✓ Learn the numbers from **1 to 10** on page 16 in the **Traveller's companion**
✓ Read today's five **New words**
✓ Read and work out the **Story**, and the **New sentences**
✓ Listen to it all on the **recording**
✓ Learn today's five **New words** and the **New sentences** by heart
✓ Take a quick look at **Nuts and bolts**. One minute will do
✓ **Let's speak German!** Now *you* do the talking
✓ Check your progress with the **recording**

The story

Paul Die Rechnung, bitte. Meine Güte! Drei Kaffee und ein Glühwein. Zehn Euro. Das ist teuer.

(Im Bus)

Claire Zwei Fahrkarten nach München, bitte. Acht Euro? Danke.

Elke Entschuldigen Sie, Claire, ich habe kein Geld. Haben Sie vier Euro, bitte?

Today's new words

die Rechnung	*the bill*
meine Güte!	*Good grief!*
der Kaffee	*coffee(s)*
die Fahrkarte, Fahrkarten	*ticket, tickets*
danke, vielen Dank	*thank you, thank you very much*

Today's new sentences

Meine Güte! Eine Fahrkarte nach Frankfurt ist billig. Zehn Euro. Ich möchte zwei. Vier Kaffee und die Rechnung, bitte. Sechs Euro. Vielen Dank.

Nuts and bolts

1 Euro – 10 Euro. No 's' at the end of **euro**!

Let's speak German!

1 Make up six German sentences. Each one must contain the two given words.

Like this: **Freundin – nicht:** Pauls **Freundin** ist **nicht** in England.

Now over to you:
- Fahrkarte – Euro
- Rechnung – haben
- Bus – vielleicht
- Leute – wo
- kein – danke
- Kaffee – oder

2 Numbers
Do you know the numbers up to 10? Then count up from 1 using these words:

Kaffee, Taxis, Fahrkarten, Berge, Autos, Häuser (houses), Rechnungen, Stunden, Busse, Freunde.

I'll start you off: Ein (*not* eins) Kaffee, zwei Fahrkarten, drei … As you can see the endings of the words for more than one thing are all over the place: Häuser! Busse! But saying them out loud will help you remember them.

Day 7

What to do today

First, here's the whole story for you to read once more – OUT LOUD. Then just work through the exercises that follow and collect your gold star at the end!

Here's this week's whole story …

Paul	Wo ist Elke?
Claire	Elke ist nicht hier. Aber viele Leute.
Paul	Das gefällt mir nicht. Wir nehmen den Bus. Einen Moment, Elke ist vielleicht hier rechts.
Claire	Nein, sie ist nicht hier. Nehmen wir ein Taxi?
Paul	Nein, wir nehmen den Bus. Entschuldigen Sie, wo ist der Bus hier nach München?
Elke	Der Bus nach München ist hier links. Aber … sind Sie nicht Paul? Ich bin Elke!
Paul	Hallo Elke, ja ich bin Paul. Und hier ist Claire.
Elke	Hallo Claire. Wie geht's? Gut? Es tut mir leid, aber ich habe kein Auto. Das Auto ist kaputt. Wir nehmen den Bus … in zwei Stunden.
Claire	In zwei Stunden? Wo ist ein Café oder eine Bar? Ich möchte einen Schnaps.
Paul	Einen Schnaps? Nein! Zwei Cappuccino, bitte. Und Sie, Elke? Möchten Sie einen Cappuccino?
Elke	Ja, bitte, und vielleicht … einen Glühwein …
Paul	Die Rechnung, bitte. Meine Güte! Drei Kaffee und ein Glühwein. Zehn Euro. Das ist teuer.

(Im Bus)

Claire	Zwei Fahrkarten nach München, bitte. Acht Euro? Danke.
Elke	Entschuldigen Sie, Claire, ich habe kein Geld. Haben Sie vier Euro, bitte?

Now you do the talking!
Tell me, tell me (in German!) that …

… Elke is the girlfriend of Helmut, … she does not have a car, … the car is out of order, … it is at Gunter's in Mannheim.

… there are a lot of people in the cafeteria (im Café) on the left, … but that there are not a lot of people in the cafeteria on the right.
… Claire wants a Cognac, … Paul does not want a Cognac, … he wants a coffee. … coffee is expensive.
… the tickets for the bus are four euros, but Elke does not have a ticket and she does not have (any) money.

Tell me about yourself

Tell me your name. Tell me you like Germany. Tell me you have six friends in Germany, they have a hotel in Hamburg. Tell me you have a ticket to Berlin in May. Tell me you would like a good hotel in Berlin, but it is not cheap. Tell me you like the hotel and you like the coffee in Germany. Tell me you would like a car in Berlin and that you would like lots of friends.

Say it in a flash

Now take out the **Flash sentences** for Week 2 with the English facing you. Say each sentence in German and then check. Give yourself three points for each one that you get right. Subtract one point for each mistake. Write down your total points at the end. Did you score 15?

A month to remember

Say out loud the names of any five months you can remember. Then write them down. Check in the **Traveller's companion** and earn yourself up to ten points, two for each that you get right. The spelling is not important as long as you can say the word correctly.

Nuts and bolts stuff

Finally here's a rare written test. Change these five lines into German, filling in the gaps with words you have learned so far. Then check with the book to see if you are correct. You can choose *and* or *but*.

• I am in _____. I have _____ and/but I would like _____.
• You are in _____. You have _____ and/but you would like _____.
• He is in _____. He has _____ and/but he would like _____.

- We are in _____. We have _____ and/but we would like _____.

- They are in _____. They have _____ and/but they would like _____.

Here's an example:

Ich bin <u>in Frankfurt</u>. Ich habe viel Geld und ich möchte ein Taxi.

Now listen to the **recording**, first to the whole **Story** and then to **Tell me, tell me** and **Tell me about yourself**. How well did you do when *you* did the talking? What did you score? Give yourself ten points for *fair*, 20 points for *good* and 25 points for *very good* for each of these exercises. And don't be modest.

For **Nuts and bolts stuff** give yourself five points for every correct line. Take off one point for each mistake.

Your result this week

Now add up all your points:

✓ Tell me, tell me ...	/25
✓ Tell me about yourself	/25
✓ Say it in a flash	/15
✓ A month to remember	/10
✓ Nuts and bolts stuff	/25

Total score this week /100% **Date** _____

What did you get ... 80%? 90%? 95%? ... 100%? Are you pleased with your score? Then enter it on the **Progress chart** on page ix.

week 03

ich möchte ein Auto kaufen

Auto kaufen

I want to buy a car

The story continues …

This is Munich! Lovely old buildings, art galleries and music, good restaurants and shops. And lots of great cars. So why not cash in those savings and get a nice little BMW? Let's ask Helmut for the name of an Autohaus …

Day 1

What to do today

✓ **Nuts and bolts:** Listen to the **recording**, then read and … learn them.

✓ Look at the **Traveller's companion**. Learn the essential verbs **gehen** *to go* and **kaufen** *to buy* on pages 20 and 22. You know most of this already

✓ Read and work out the **Story**, today's five **New words** and the **New sentences**

✓ Learn today's five **New words** and the **New sentences** by heart

✓ **Let's speak German!** Do the two exercises to practise speaking OUT LOUD

✓ Check your progress with the **recording**

The story

Claire **Helmut, eine Frage, bitte. Gibt es hier ein Autohaus? Ich möchte einen BMW kaufen.**

Helmut **Ein BMW kostet viel Geld! Ein Autohaus? Mmm. Vielleicht Autohaus Becker, oder Graaf. Ja, Autohaus Graaf.**

Today's new words

eine Frage	*a question*
es gibt, gibt es?	*there is/are, is there/are there?*
ein Autohaus	lit: *a car house = a car dealer*
kaufen	*to buy*
kostet	*costs*

Today's new sentences

Ich möchte einen Mercedes kaufen. Was kostet ein Mercedes? Gibt es hier ein gutes Autohaus?

Nuts and bolts

Splitting the action

Germans like to keep you in suspense …

When Claire says: **Ich möchte einen BMW kaufen** you don't know until the end of the sentence what she would like to do to the BMW – sell it, buy it, wash it, or smash it up?

Here's the rule: When there are two action words – verbs – the second one goes right to the end of the sentence. So you have to re-think and say to yourself: I would like a BMW …. buy. Once you have done this a few times it gets quite easy.

Here's another example: I would not like to fly in June to New York. Re-think: I would not like in June to New York … fly. **Ich möchte nicht im Juni nach New York … fliegen.**

Got it?

Let's speak German!

1 Say these sentences in German – and remember to split the action!

- Helmut would like to buy a Mercedes in Stuttgart.
- Claire goes to buy a ticket.
- We would like to have a house in Florida.
- Would you like to fly to Frankfurt in November?
- He would not like to have a lot of money in America.
- She would like to have many friends in Berlin.
- I am going (I go) to buy coffee.

2 Now answer in German:

- Wieviel (how much) kostet der Kaffee?
- Gibt es eine Rechnung?
- Wo gibt es hier Fahrkarten?
- Wieviel kosten die Fahrkarten?
- Gibt es in Kiel viel Schnee im Dezember?
- Wieviel kostet ein Hotel in Hamburg?

Day 2

What to do today

✓ Read today's five **New words**
✓ Read and work out today's **Story** and the **New sentences**
✓ Listen and speak along with the **recording**
✓ Learn today's five **New words** and the **New sentences** by heart
✓ Practise speaking with **Let's speak German!**
✓ Check your progress with the **recording**

The story

Paul   Hallo Helmut. Ich habe eine Frage: Ich möchte ein Auto kaufen. Mein Auto in England ist kaputt … Ich möchte einen VW oder vielleicht einen BMW. Der BMW gefällt mir. Wo gibt es hier ein Autohaus?

Helmut   Es gibt ein Autohaus für BMW im Zentrum. Graaf sind sehr gut.

Today's new words

mein, meine	*my*
das Zentrum, im Zentrum	*the centre, in the centre*
für	*for*
sind	*are*
sehr	*very*

Today's new sentences

Eine Frage: Gibt es hier ein Café im Zentrum? Die Cafés in Berlin sind sehr gut. Ich möchte Kaffee für vier. Aber wo ist mein Geld?

Let's speak German!

1 Say these sentences in German:

- I would like a bus for the centre.
- Mercedes and BMW are very good cars, but expensive.
- I would like to take my car and go to Paris.
- I have a question: Are there a lot of good restaurants in the centre?

2 And here's another practice round on **sein**, **möchten**, **gehen** and **kaufen**.

Say in German:

- I go to the bus, he goes to the car.
- I am in (on) the bus, he is in the car.
- I would like to go to the café, he would like to go to the taxi.
- I am Claire's (female) friend, she is Paul's friend.
- I go skiing, he does not go skiing.
- I am buying (buy) a coffee, he is buying (buys) a schnapps.

Day 3

What to do today

✓ Read today's five **New words**
✓ Read and work out the **Story**, and the **New sentences**
✓ Listen to and speak along with the **recording**
✓ Look at the **Traveller's companion** and learn the essential verbs **haben** (to have) and **nehmen** (to take) on pages 20 and 22. You know most of them already
✓ Learn the **Nuts and bolts** and listen to the **recording**
✓ Learn today's five **New words** and the **New sentences** by heart. Are you using the **Flash cards**?
✓ **Let's speak German!** *You* are doing the talking!
✓ Check your progress with the **recording**

The story

Claire (*On the phone*) **Guten Tag, Autohaus Graaf? Ich bin Claire Smith ... Nein, nicht Klärmis. Claire – Smith ... Das macht nichts. Ich bin hier in München, und ich möchte ein Auto kaufen ... Ich möchte einen Termin ... Ja, morgen ist gut. Mit Herrn Becker.**

Today's new words

guten Tag	*good day*
das macht nichts	*it doesn't matter*
ein Termin	*an appointment*
morgen	*tomorrow*
mit	*with*

Today's new sentences

Guten Tag. Ich möchte einen Termin mit Ilse. Haben Sie einen Termin für morgen? Wo ist sie morgen? Im Zentrum. Das macht nichts.

Nuts and bolts

mit – *with*, für – *for*

These two harmless looking words cause a lot of havoc. After **mit** all the alarm bells start ringing, because:

der changes to **dem**
die changes to **der**
das changes to **dem**

… and if you use **die** for more than one thing this changes to **den**!

Mit also changes the endings of other little words, like *my*. But don't throw the book away. Just try to remember a few combinations and forget about the rest. It's not that serious.

Der Freund, mein Freund – but: **mit dem** Freund, **mit meinem** Freund.
Die Fahrkarte, meine Fahrkarte – but: **mit der** Fahrkarte, **mit meiner** Fahrkarte.
Das Auto, mein Auto – but: **mit dem** Auto, **mit meinem** Auto.
Die Leute – but: **mit den** Leuten.

für *for*

This is another troublemaker, but a small one. It only changes **der** into **den**.

der Freund, mein Freund – but: **für den** Freund, **für meinen** Freund.

Let's speak German!

1 Add the missing bits to complete the sentences.

- Morgen _____ wir ein neues Auto.
- Ist es kaputt? Das _____ nichts.
- Guten _____, entschuldigen _____, gibt es hier Fahrkarten?
- Ich habe einen _____ in zwei Stunden.
- Der Termin ist _____ dem Autohaus.

2 Now make up five sentences, all starting with **morgen**. Use any form of **kaufen**, **haben**, **möchten**, **nehmen** and **gehen** and use either **für** or **mit** in the sentence. Just for once write down what you say. When you've checked your work then say each sentence – out loud – with your eyes closed. Remember what happens to the action word after starting with **morgen** …

- Morgen …
- Morgen …
- Morgen …
- Morgen …
- Morgen …

Day 4

What to do today

✓ Read today's five **New words**
✓ Read and work out the **Story** and the **New sentences**. Then listen to it all on the **recording**
✓ Learn today's five **New words** and the **New sentences** by heart
✓ Look at the **Traveller's companion**. On page 9 you'll find **Useful places and services** – something Paul and Claire might need if they are buying that new car …
✓ **Let's speak German!** Enjoy the two speaking exercises
✓ Check your progress with the **recording**

The story

Paul *(on the phone)* **Hallo, Autohaus Graaf? Mein Name ist Blair. Nein, nicht Tony. Paul, Paul Blair. Ich bin hier im Urlaub, von Birmingham, mit meiner Frau, und ich möchte ein Auto kaufen. Haben Sie einen Termin, heute oder morgen? … Ja, danke.**

Today's new words

der Name	*the name*
im Urlaub	*on holiday*
von	*from, of*
meine Frau, mit meiner Frau	*my wife, with my wife*
heute	*today*

Today's new sentences

Mein Name ist Schmidt. Ich habe Urlaub. Ich bin hier mit Claire. Das ist meine Frau. Wir fahren morgen von Hamburg nach Düsseldorf.

Let's speak German!

Have another quick look at the places of interest in the **Traveller's companion**. Then tell me in German that …

• The post office and the bank are in the centre.
• The department store is very good but expensive.

- You like the church.
- Tomorrow you are going to the (zur) petrol station.
- You have a question for the tourist office.
- It is two hours from the museum to the (zum) hospital.
- You don't like the cinema.
- You would like the police.

Speed test

Say these sentences as quickly as you can:

- Ich möchte eine Fahrkarte.
- Ich möchte eine Fahrkarte für zehn Euro.
- Ich möchte eine Fahrkarte für zehn Euro von Hamburg nach Hannover.

- Gibt es hier eine Bank?
- Gibt es hier eine Deutsche Bank?
- Gibt es hier eine Deutsche Bank und eine Post?
- Gibt es hier links oder rechts eine Deutsche Bank und eine Post?

- Wieviel kostet das?
- Wieviel Geld kostet das Auto?
- Wieviel Geld kostet das Auto für meine Frau?
- Wieviel Geld kostet das Auto für meine Frau im Autohaus im Zentrum – in Euro?

Day 5

What to do today

✓ Read today's five **New words**
✓ Read and work out the **Story** and the **New sentences**
✓ Listen and speak along with the **recording**
✓ **Nuts and bolts:** Listen to the **recording**, then read and learn them
✓ Learn today's five **New words** and the **New sentences** by heart
✓ Look at the **Traveller's companion**. There are some **shopping hints** on page 6, just in case you need to flash your credit card …
✓ **Let's speak German!** … and do the two speaking exercises

Nuts and bolts

The story

Claire Hallo Helmut, ich gehe einkaufen. Kann ich bitte das Auto haben? Ich möchte zum Zentrum. Wo ist Paul?

Helmut Er ist bei meinem Auto. Es gibt ein Problem. Das Auto hat immer ein Problem.

Today's new words

ich gehe einkaufen	*I am going shopping*
ich kann, kann ich?	*I can, can I?*
zu, zum, zur	*to, to the*
ein Problem	*a problem*
immer	*always*

Today's new sentences

Ich gehe morgen einkaufen, mit meinem Freund. Wir fahren zum Zentrum von München. Mein Freund möchte bei Graaf ein Auto kaufen. Aber er hat immer ein Problem: Er hat kein Geld.

1 Remember **mit**? The little word which caused havoc? Here's some bad news: He's got friends! **Bei**, **von** and **zu** create exactly the same problems. But as I said before, pick up what you can and ignore the rest. Mistakes won't spoil your success. Everyone will still understand you perfectly.

2 heute and morgen

In everyday German there is no difference between the verb which tells you that you are doing something today, or in the future.

Ich **gehe** heute **einkaufen**. – Ich **gehe** morgen **einkaufen**.

3 I would like to go shopping.

In German you say: *I would like to shopping go*. – **Ich möchte einkaufen gehen**.

Don't blame me!

Let's speak German!

1 Read the questions and then answer in German.

- Möchten Sie heute einkaufen gehen?
  Say that you would like to go shopping today and that you always buy coffee in Germany.
- Ich fliege heute nach London. Und Sie?
  Say that you are on holiday but that you can fly to Berlin tomorrow.
- Ich habe ein Problem mit meinem Haus. Und Sie?
  Say that you always have a problem with your house and that it costs a lot of money.

2 You are in a department store. Tell me in four sentences what clothes you and other people are buying. You can look at page 6 of the **Traveller's companion** to refresh your memory. Here is an example:

Ich kaufe ein Kleid. Meine Freundin kauft Schuhe.

Use: **viele Leute**, **Erich**, **mein Freund**, **Ilse** plus **eine Hose**, **eine Jacke**, **einen Mantel**, **einen Pullover**, **ein Kostüm**, **eine Strumpfhose**, **ein Hemd**, **einen Regenschirm**.

Day 6

What to do today

✓ Read today's five **New words**
✓ Read and work out the **Story** and the **New sentences**. Listen and speak with the **recording**
✓ Learn today's five **New words** and the **New sentences** by heart
✓ Speak in a flash: Take out the five **Flash sentences** and, with the English side facing you, say the five sentences in German until you are word perfect
✓ Get out the **Traveller's companion**: If you are a serious shopper there is more to read on page 7
✓ **Let's speak German!** That means *you*!
✓ Check your progress with the **recording**

The story

Herr Becker	**Guten Tag, Frau Smith. Ich bin Rolf Becker. Sie sind hier im Urlaub von Birmingham und möchten einen neuen BMW kaufen, ja? Entschuldigen Sie, einen Moment bitte. Hier ist auch jemand von Birmingham, ein Herr Blair. Er möchte auch einen BMW kaufen.**
Paul	**Claire! Meine Güte!**
Herr Becker	**Entschuldigen Sie, möchten Sie einen BMW oder zwei?**

Today's new words

Frau	*Mrs*
neu, neuen	*new*
auch	*also*
jemand	*someone*
Herr	*Mr*

Today's new sentences

Frau Smith möchte ein neues Auto. Sie möchte einen VW, aber Herr Blair möchte einen Mercedes. Jemand möchte einen Ferrari. Sie auch?

Let's speak German!

Quick shopping drill

1 Say in German:

- I go shopping.
- I go shopping with Frau Meyer.
- Tomorrow I'll go shopping.
- Tomorrow I'll go shopping with Frau Meyer.
- I would like to go shopping.
- I would like to go shopping with Frau Meyer.
- Tomorrow I would like to go shopping with Frau Meyer.

2 Read these sentences out loud and answer in German, starting with **nein**.

- Frau Schulze ist im Urlaub und geht heute bei Karstadt einkaufen. Sie auch?
- Herr Zimmermann geht morgen zur Bank und zum Reisebüro. Er möchte nach Österreich (Austria) fliegen. Sie auch?
- Frau Schmidt ist neu in Hamburg und möchte eine billige Fahrkarte nach Berlin kaufen. Sie auch?
- Jemand hat ein Problem und möchte einen Termin bei der Polizei. Sie auch?

Day 7

Today you get a break from learning: no **New words** or **New sentences**. Today it's time for you to assess your progress.

What to do today

✓ Read this week's complete **Story** out loud. It has a word count of over 200 words!

✓ Have a go at the exercises that follow

Here's the week's whole story ...

Claire	Helmut, eine Frage, bitte. Gibt es hier ein Autohaus? Ich möchte einen BMW kaufen.
Helmut	Ein BMW kostet viel Geld! Ein Autohaus? Mmm. Vielleicht Autohaus Becker, oder Graaf. Ja, Autohaus Graaf.
Paul	Hallo Helmut. Ich habe eine Frage: Ich möchte ein Auto kaufen. Mein Auto in England ist kaputt ... Ich möchte einen VW oder vielleicht einen BMW. Der BMW gefällt mir. Wo gibt es hier ein Autohaus?
Helmut	Es gibt ein Autohaus für BMW im Zentrum. Graaf sind sehr gut.
Claire	*(on the phone)* Guten Tag, Autohaus Graaf? Ich bin Claire Smith ... Nein, nicht Klärmis. Claire – Smith ... Das macht nichts. Ich bin hier in München, und ich möchte ein Auto kaufen ... Ich möchte einen Termin ... Ja, morgen ist gut. Mit Herrn Becker.
Paul	*(on the phone)* Hallo, Autohaus Graaf? Mein Name ist Blair. Nein, nicht Tony. Paul, Paul Blair. Ich bin hier im Urlaub, von Birmingham, mit meiner Frau, und ich möchte ein Auto kaufen. Haben Sie einen Termin, heute oder morgen? ... Ja, danke.
Claire	Hallo Helmut, ich gehe einkaufen. Kann ich, bitte das Auto haben? Ich möchte zum Zentrum. Wo ist Paul?
Helmut	Er ist bei meinem Auto. Es gibt ein Problem. Das Auto hat immer ein Problem.

Herr Becker	Guten Tag, Frau Smith. Ich bin Rolf Becker. Sie sind hier im Urlaub von Birmingham und möchten einen neuen BMW kaufen, ja? Entschuldigen Sie, einen Moment, bitte. Hier ist auch jemand von Birmingham, ein Herr Blair. Er möchte auch einen BMW kaufen.
Paul	Claire! Meine Güte!
Herr Becker	Entschuldigen Sie, möchten Sie einen BMW oder zwei?

This is the day that *you* do all the talking. Here goes:

Tell me, tell me …

Tell me it is July and that you are on holiday in Germany. Tell me you have the name of a car dealer and that you would like to buy a car. Tell me you have an appointment for tomorrow with Herrn Huber.

Tell me that you like the coffee in Germany and that a Cappuccino is not expensive, perhaps one euro or two. Tell me you like the centre of Munich and that there are always a lot of people in the Hofbräuhaus*. Tell me you do not have many euros, but that it doesn't matter. You don't have a problem.

*famous Munich beer garden

Now tell me about Julie …

Tell me that you have a friend, Julie. Tell me she is from Manchester, she does not have a car, she goes by bus. She would like to go to Germany with a friend. Tell me the friend has a lot of money and a lot of friends in Frankfurt; they have tickets (here: Flugkarten) for August. Tell me Julie would like to buy two jerseys: they are good and not very expensive in Germany.

Remember the numbers?

Try to say the numbers from one to ten. Only after you have said them write them down – the way you said them. Now check them against the **Traveller's companion**, page 16, and give yourself a point for every one you got right. The spelling is not important.

How's your memory?

Take out all 90 **Flash words** for Weeks 1 to 3. Shuffle them and pick out (without looking) any 25. Now, with the English side facing you, say the German and give yourself one point for every word you know immediately. Score 25 points for knowing them all.

Remember the words?

Give me five places of interest and five items of clothing. Score one point for each one you remember and can say out loud.

Now listen to the **recording**. First to the whole story and then to **Tell me, tell me …** and then to **Tell me about Julie**.

Give yourself between 10 and 25 points for each of the three speaking exercises, depending on how well you did.

Your result this week

Add up all your points:

✓ Tell me, tell me …	/25
✓ Tell me about Julie	/25
✓ Remember the numbers?	/10
✓ How's your memory?	/25
✓ Remember the words?	/10
Total score	**/100%** **Date** _____

I'll bet you scored more than 70%! Now enter your result on the **Progress chart**.

Österreich
wir fahren nach

we are going to Austria

The story continues …

Paul and Claire are off to Austria in Helmut's old car. The snow is good and the skiing is great. But later that day, after a couple of drinks, will they find a place to stay?

Day 1

What to do today

- ✓ Read today's **New words**
- ✓ Read and work out the **Story** and the **New sentences**
- ✓ Learn the **New words** and **New sentences** by heart
- ✓ Listen and speak along with the **recording**
- ✓ Look at the **Traveller's companion**. Take a look at **Getting about, not lost** on page 8
- ✓ **Let's speak German!** Over to you
- ✓ Check your progress with the **recording**

The story

Paul   Ich möchte für eine Nacht nach Salzburg. Ich möchte Berge und Schnee sehen.

Claire   Und ich möchte Ski fahren. Was nehmen wir – das Auto, einen Bus oder den Zug? Und wann?

Today's new words

eine Nacht	*one night*
sehen	*see, to see*
was	*what*
der Zug	*the train*
wann?	*when?*

Today's new sentences

Ich möchte den Schwarzwald* sehen. Wie ist der Schwarzwald? Toll! Fliegen wir nach Stuttgart? Nein, wir nehmen den Zug.

* the Black Forest

Let's speak German!

1   Answer the questions below using *all* the following words:

für eine Nacht, **beim Hofbräuhaus**, **im September**, **100 (hundert) Euro**, **mit dem Zug**, **im Schnee**, **von London**, **den Schwarzwald**, **vielleicht**, **hier links**, **für zwei**, **im Zentrum**

- Was möchten Sie sehen?
- Wann fliegen Sie nach Zürich?

- Wo ist der Bahnhof?
- Wieviel kostet das Hotel?
- Wie fahren Sie nach Deutschland?

2 Here are some answers. Ask the questions which give you these answers.

- Ja, ich kann morgen das Auto kaufen.
- Nein, ich kann die Haltestelle nicht sehen.
- Ja, ich kann immer im Mai Urlaub haben.
- Nein, ich kann heute nicht einkaufen gehen.
- Ja, ich kann zwei Stunden mit der U-Bahn fahren.

Day 2

What to do today

✓ Read today's **New words**
✓ Read and work out the **Story** and the **New sentences**
✓ Listen and speak along with the **recording**
✓ Learn today's five **New words** and the **New sentences** by heart
✓ Take a look at the verbs **brauchen** and **können** in the **Traveller's companion**, pages 21 and 22
✓ **Nuts and bolts:** Listen to the **recording**, then read and learn them
✓ **Let's speak German!** Speak OUT LOUD
✓ Check your progress with the **recording**

The story

Paul **Wenn wir heute fahren, können wir das Auto nehmen. Denn Helmut braucht es heute nicht.**
Claire **Gut, wir fahren heute!**

Today's new words

wenn	*if*
wir können	*we can*
denn	*because*
braucht	*needs*
es	*it*

Today's new sentences

Wenn wir nach Frankfurt fahren, können wir den Zug nehmen. Wir brauchen keinen Zug. Wir können mit dem Auto fahren. Wann? Um acht. Denn wir möchten viel sehen.

Nuts and bolts

wenn *if*

If a sentence starts with **wenn** the action word – the verb – goes right to the end of that part of the sentence. In the second part of the sentence the verb rushes to the front. Like this:

If I have a lot of money I buy a car. **Wenn** ich viel Geld **habe**, **kaufe** ich ein Auto.

because

There are two words in German which mean *because*: **denn** and **weil**. I have chosen the easy one – **denn**. If you use **weil** you would have to remember to move the verb to the end again, like this:

> Ich nehme den Zug, **denn** ich **habe** eine Fahrkarte.
> Ich nehme den Zug, **weil** ich eine Fahrkarte **habe**.

If in doubt use **denn**!

Let's speak German!

1 Practise saying **denn** – *because,* and replace the English with the German. If you are ambitious try **weil** afterwards! We'll give you both in the answers.

- Ich fahre nicht nach Bremen *because I don't like it.*
- *I don't have a car because* es gibt einen sehr guten Bus.
- Ich gehe nicht in ein Luxushotel *because it is expensive*.
- Wir fliegen nach Stuttgart *because we have a friend in the Black Forest*.
- Wir kaufen viel Wein *because we are on holiday*.

2 brauchen and **können**

Say in German:
I need the train to Berlin, you can take the car, he can see lots of people, she needs a friend, we need someone here, they need tickets, it cannot be.

3 Now complete the missing part of the sentence and practise *if*.

- *If I don't have money for a taxi*, fahre ich mit dem Bus.
- *If we buy the house today*, kostet es nicht viel Geld.
- Wenn er nach Frankfurt möchte, *he needs a car*.
- Wenn wir nach Deutschland fahren, *we can buy a Mercedes in Stuttgart*.

Day 3

What to do today

✓ Read today's **New words**
✓ Read and work out the **Story** and the **New sentences**
✓ Read the **Nuts and bolts**
✓ Take out the **Traveller's companion**. Have a look at the **colours** on page 17. Try to read them out loud twice. They'll be repeated for you shortly on the **recording**
✓ Learn today's five **New words** and the **New sentences** by heart
✓ Listen and speak along with the **recording**
✓ **Let's speak German!** Now *you* do the talking!
✓ Check your progress with the **recording**

The story

Claire **Der Schnee ist toll. Ski fahren gefällt mir sehr.**
Paul **Und das Bier gefällt mir auch.**
Claire **Ein Glas Weisswein für mich, bitte. Und wo sind die Toiletten?**

Today's new words

Bier	*beer*
ein Glas	*a glass*
Weisswein, Rotwein	*white wine, red wine*
für mich	*for me*
die Toiletten	*the toilets*

Today's new sentences

Ich möchte ein Glas Bier, bitte. Für mich ein Glas Rotwein. Entschuldigen Sie, gibt es hier Toiletten?

Nuts and bolts

Colours and other adjectives

These are easy to learn. Many are similar to the English. For example:

weiss – white **braun** – brown **gut** – good **grün** – green

So it's: *the coffee is cheap, the question is good, the house is brown* or *the cars are green*: **Der Kaffee ist billig, die Frage ist gut, das Haus ist braun, die Autos sind grün.**

The trouble starts when you want to say: *the cheap coffee* or *the good question*. You now add an **-e** to the end of the adjective or **-en** if you are talking about more than one thing. So it's: das braun**e** Haus, die grün**en** Autos.

Now that's not too bad. But try to say: *a cheap coffee, a good question*, *a brown house* or *green cars*. Here we go:

der Kaffee, **ein** billig**er** Kaffee
die Frage, **eine** gut**e** Frage
das Haus, **ein** braun**es** Haus
die Autos, grün**e** Autos

But now for the good news: This is a **Starter kit** to get you to *speak* German, not pass exams. Correct endings (like word order) are optional. It's great if you remember some, but they are not part of the programme.

Let's speak German!

Say in German:

- The car is red and broken down.
- I like the expensive white car.
- Excuse me, are there toilets here on the right?
- Does someone have my ticket for the train?
- Yes, a ticket for me.
- Would you like a glass of red wine?
- No, thank you very much, for me a beer, please.
- If you have white wine, I'll take a glass please.
- I would like a glass of beer, because the wine is very expensive.

Day 4

What to do today

✓ **Nuts and bolts**: Listen to the **recording**, then read and learn them
✓ Look at the **Traveller's companion**. On page 19 you'll find some **Communication essentials**, like *hello*, *excuse me*, *thank you*, *good bye*, and many more. Have a good read through
✓ Read today's **New words**
✓ Read and work out the **Story** and the **New sentences**
✓ Listen and speak along with the **recording**
✓ Learn today's five **New words** and the **New sentences** by heart
✓ **Let's speak German!** Do the three speaking exercises
✓ Check your progress with the **recording**

The story

(Several drinks later they are looking for a hotel …)

Claire **Wir müssen jetzt ein Hotel suchen**. *(Turning to a stranger)* **Entschuldigen Sie, können Sie mir bitte helfen? Wir suchen ein Hotel.**

Today's new words

wir müssen	*we must*
jetzt	*now*
ein Hotel	*a hotel*
suchen	*to look for*
Können Sie mir bitte helfen?	*Can you help me, please?*

Today's new sentences

Entschuldigen Sie, können Sie mir bitte helfen? Wir suchen einen Bus zum Zentrum. Und wo müssen wir die Fahrkarten kaufen?

Nuts and bolts

müssen and **muss**
Only two words to cover all. Easy! Have a look in the **Traveller's companion** and look at the list on page 24.

Remember: if you must *go* somewhere you leave out the *go*.

I must go to the bus.   **Ich muss zum Bus**.

Let's speak German!

Never skip the **New sentences**. If you haven't done so today learn the three sentences by heart now. You never know when you may need one of them.

1 I must …

Pretend you want to get out of a boring invitation. Make up some excuses starting with: **Es tut mir leid aber ich muss …
und dann** (and then) **muss ich …**

Now add: **Ich muss nach … und dann muss ich … kaufen,
und dann muss ich nach** (name of town).

2 Ask someone these questions in German: **Müssen Sie … ?**

• Do you have to look for the ticket?
• Do you have to go shopping?
• Do you have to buy the coffee?
• Do you have (to go) to Aachen?
• Do you have to have the car?
• Do you have to take the money?

3 Back to the **Traveller's companion**. Pick out four favourites from the **Communication essentials** on page 19 and build four sentences around them. Say these sentences OUT LOUD. Afterwards you can write them down if you want to.

Day 5

What to do today

✓ Read today's **New words**
✓ Read and work out the **Story** and the **New sentences**
✓ Listen and speak along with the **recording**
✓ **Nuts and bolts**: Listen to the **recording**, then read and learn them
✓ Learn today's five **New words** and the **New sentences** by heart
✓ **Let's speak German!** Speaking practice for you
✓ Check your progress with the **recording**

The story

Gary **Hotel? Me English. Gutes Hotel hier, close by. Sehr billig. But cash only, no Kreditkarten. Where's a Geldautomat? No idea. Sorry, must dash. Cheers.**

Paul **Wir haben kein Bargeld, und wir können nicht Auto fahren. Nicht nach fünf Glas Bier. Wo ist das Handy? Wir rufen ein Hotel an.**

Today's new words

eine Kreditkarte, Kreditkarten	*a credit card, credit cards*
ein Geldautomat	*a cash dispenser*
Bargeld	*cash*
das Handy	*the mobile phone*
anrufen	*to call (by phone)*

Today's new sentences

Ich muss ein Hotel anrufen. Ich habe kein Handy. Ich brauche Bargeld. Ich suche einen Geldautomaten. Ich habe kein Auto. Meine Güte!

Nuts and bolts

anrufen

This action word is often split into two parts: **an** + **rufen**. When you use **anrufen** in a sentence it is split up like this:

Ich **rufe** meinen Freund **an**. Morgen **rufen** wir das Autohaus **an**.

But when you use **anrufen** with *another* action word like **können** or **müssen**, it stays intact:

Ich muss **anrufen**. Möchten Sie das Hotel **anrufen**?

And if you forget and say … **Morgen wir anrufen das Autohaus … ?** You might get two black marks from the academics but any German would still understand you perfectly.

Let's speak German!

1 Say in German:

- I don't have a mobile phone. Can you phone the hotel, please?
- We cannot call the hotel. We are calling Paul's house.
- Where are the credit cards? We must call the bank today.
- The ATM on the right is out of order.
- Do you have a credit card?

2 More practice of **if** and **because**

Say these sentences in German:

- If you want cash you need an ATM.
- If I go shopping I must have a lot of money.
- If you must (go) to Hamburg you must fly in two hours.
- I need my credit card because I don't have (any) cash.
- We are looking for an ATM because we want to buy tickets.
- Can you help me, please, because my car has broken down.

Day 6

What to do today

- ✓ Read today's five **New words**
- ✓ Read and work out the **Story** and the **New sentences**
- ✓ Listen and speak along with the **recording**
- ✓ Learn today's five **New words** and the **New sentences** by heart
- ✓ Take out the **Traveller's companion**: it's time for two more essential verbs. Look at **fahren** and **wollen** on pages 21 and 23. Then turn back to page 17 and have a look at **the days of the week**
- ✓ **Let's speak German!** Over to you
- ✓ Check your progress with the **recording**

The story

Claire   **Es gibt hier ein Schlosshotel. Ich liebe gute Hotels.**

Paul   *(on the phone)* **Hallo. Ist das das Schlosshotel? Guten Tag. Haben Sie ein Doppelzimmer für eine Nacht? ... Ja, für heute ... Wieviel kostet das? ... Was ... ? Wieviel? Hmmmm ... danke. Meine Güte! Ich will das Zimmer nicht *kaufen*!**

Today's new words

das Schloss,	*the castle*
ein Schlosshotel	*a palace hotel/stately home*
ich liebe	*I love*
ein Zimmer, Doppelzimmer	*a room, double room*
Wieviel kostet das?	*How much does that cost?*
ich will	*I want, I want to*

Today's new sentences

Wir möchten ein Zimmer für eine Nacht, aber nicht teuer. Was kostet das? Hotel Meier ist gut und billig. Hmm ... Das gefällt mir nicht. Was wollen Sie? Ein Schloss?

Let's speak German!

1 Question time: **was? wann? wieviel? wie? wo?**

Ask these questions in German, then answer them in German – in whole sentences – using the words in brackets.

* What does Claire want? *(a palace hotel)*
* When do you have (to go) to *(today)*
  Berlin, today or tomorrow?
* How much is a double room? *(100 (hundert)*
  euros for two)
* How is the centre of Munich? *(great)*
* Where are you on holiday in August? *(in Austria)*

2 Here's someone who loves *everything*. She loves … the room, the question, the train, the castle, the people, and the white wine. She would say: **Ich liebe …** (then say all the things she loves).

3 On the move …

Use **fahren** for *go* to make it clear that you are using transport (not your feet). Say these phrases in German:

I go on Monday, you go on Tuesday, does Gerhard go on Wednesday? Heidi goes on Thursday, we go on Friday, they go on Saturday, and … I do not go on Sunday.

Note: In German you say: I go *on the* Monday: **Ich fahre *am* Montag**

Now do the exercise again saying … *I want to go …* Ich **will** am Montag **fahren**.

Day 7

Today you are going to mark up your **Progress chart** and see how well you are doing. But first there's a little work to be done …

What to do today

✓ Read the complete **Story** OUT LOUD
✓ Do the four speaking exercises that follow and work out your score

Here's this week's whole story …

Paul Ich möchte für eine Nacht nach Salzburg. Ich möchte Berge und Schnee sehen.

Claire Und ich möchte Ski fahren. Was nehmen wir – das Auto, einen Bus oder den Zug? Und wann?

Paul Wenn wir heute fahren, können wir das Auto nehmen. Denn Helmut braucht es heute nicht.

Claire Gut, wir fahren heute! Der Schnee ist toll. Ski fahren gefällt mir sehr.

Paul Und das Bier gefällt mir auch.

Claire Ein Glas Weisswein für mich, bitte. Und wo sind die Toiletten?

(Several drinks later they are looking for a hotel …)

Claire Wir müssen jetzt ein Hotel suchen. *(Turning to a stranger)* Entschuldigen Sie, können Sie mir bitte helfen? Wir suchen ein Hotel.

Gary Hotel? Me English. Gutes Hotel hier, close by. Sehr billig. But cash only, no Kreditkarten. Where's a Geldautomat? No idea. Sorry, must dash. Cheers.

Paul Wir haben kein Bargeld, und wir können nicht Auto fahren. Nicht nach fünf Glas Bier. Wo ist das Handy? Wir rufen ein Hotel an.

Claire Es gibt hier ein Schlosshotel. Ich liebe gute Hotels.

Paul *(on the phone)* Hallo. Ist das das Schlosshotel? Guten Tag. Haben Sie ein Doppelzimmer für eine Nacht? … Ja, für heute … Wieviel kostet das? … Was … ? Wieviel? Hmmmm … danke. Meine Güte! Ich will das Zimmer nicht *kaufen*!

And now for the talking!

All the following are *speaking* exercises. If you really must write things down, don't do so *until* you have said everything OUT LOUD.

Tell me, tell me …

Tell me you would like to see Köln and the Rhine (den Rhein), you can go by train or by car because your friend has a Ferrari and he does not need the car in July. Tell me you would like to see the Mosel and that you want to see the hotels in the Black Forest. Tell me you love the white wine but that you also like the German (das deutsche) beer. Tell me you must look for a hotel or you can call your friend in Köln with your mobile phone; he has perhaps a room for a night.

Give yourself between 10 and 25 points depending on how well you can say it all.

Tell me in a flash

With the English side facing you, say the **Flash sentences** in German. And then check. Give yourself four points for every correct sentence. Take one point off for every mistake.

Speak in German

Use **müssen** *have to* and **können** *can*

- I don't have to go shopping today. I can go tomorrow.
- You don't have to buy the mobile phone. But you can if you want to.
- We don't have to go to London for seven nights. We can go for one.
- They don't have to buy the red wine. They can buy the white.
- He doesn't have to look for the cash dispenser. He can buy the tickets with a credit card.

Give yourself five points for every correct pair of sentences. Deduct a point for each mistake.

How's your memory?

Now try to remember … and say the words OUT LOUD. (Then you can write them down if you wish.)

- Five colours, like **rosa**
- Five verbs in their basic form, like **nehmen** – to take
- Five nouns, like **der Schnee**
- Five names of months like **Mai**
- Five days of the week like **Montag**
- Five communcation essentials like **hallo**

Give yourself one point for each word you remember.

Now listen to the **recording** to find out how well you have done.

Your result this week

Finally, add up all your points:

✓ Tell me, tell me … /25

✓ Tell me in a flash /20

✓ Speak in German /25

✓ How's your memory? /30

Total score **/100%** **Date** _____

Are you pleased? Don't forget to mark up your **Progress chart**.

05

im Restaurant
in the restaurant

The story continues …

When Claire goes to the supermarket she bumps into old friends, Tom and Kate. Later that evening they all go out for a meal. Ursula is their waitress, and she's got a problem …

Day 1

What to do today

✓ Read the five **New words**
✓ Read and work out the **Story** and the **New sentences**. Listen and speak along with the **recording**
✓ **Nuts and bolts**: Listen to the **recording**, then read and learn them
✓ Look at the **Traveller's companion**. There are lots of useful examples of **verbs in the past tense** on page 26
✓ Learn today's five **New words** and the **New sentences** by heart
✓ Test yourself with **Let's speak German!** Do the speaking exercise
✓ Check your progress with the **recording**

The story

Claire **Paul, hier ist etwas sehr interessantes: Ich war im Supermarkt, um Wein zu kaufen. Und ich habe zwei Freunde von London gesehen – Tom und Kate!**

Today's new words

interessant,	*interesting,*
etwas interessantes	*something interesting*
ich war	*I was*
der Supermarkt	*supermarket*
um	*in order to*
ich habe gesehen	*I have seen, I saw*

Today's new sentences

Ich war in Stuttgart, um ein Auto zu kaufen. Ich habe einen sehr interessanten Mercedes gesehen … Aber er war sehr teuer.

Nuts and bolts

the past

When you talk about something that happened before – in the past – the action word changes, just like in English.

To say that you *have done* something you use a form of **haben** plus the other verb, slightly changed and often starting with **ge-**. Here's an example:

ich habe gekauft   *I have bought*, or, *I bought*

If the sentence is a little longer the two verbs are split again, to keep you guessing, with the second verb moving to the end. Like this:

Ich *habe* heute in Bonn ein Auto (written off? stolen?) … *gekauft.*

Finally, remember what happens when the sentence does not start with the subject but with an introduction? The **haben** rushes to the front, like this:

Im Juli *habe ich* ein Auto gekauft.

Let's speak German!

Practise speaking in the past: **gesehen**, **gesucht**, **gekauft**, and **genommen** (taken) to say these sentences in German.

- Did you see the red car at the hotel?
- He saw a cheap wine at the supermarket.
- I bought a lot of beer in Germany because I love it.
- They bought four tickets for the train.
- We took the bus to the centre because the taxi was expensive.
- She looked for a palace in the Black Forest.

Day 2

What to do today

✓ Read the five **New words**
✓ Read and work out the **Story** and the **New sentences**. Speak along with the **recording**
✓ **Nuts and bolts**: Listen to the **recording**, then read and learn them
✓ Look at the **Traveller's companion**. It's time for a few more numbers. Have a look at the numbers **11 to 50** on page 16
✓ Learn today's five **New words** and the **New sentences** by heart
✓ **Let's speak German!** Don't write the answers – say them!
✓ Check your progress with the **recording**

The story

Claire **Wir sind in ein Café gegangen, und Tom hat gesagt, dass er ein schönes Auto gesehen hat. Aber Kate will es nicht. Es ist sehr teuer.**

Today's new words

wir sind gegangen	*we have gone, we went*
hat gesagt	*has said, said*
dass	*that*
schön, schönes	*beautiful*
hat gesehen/gesehen hat	*has seen, saw*

Today's new sentences

Wir sind heute ins Zentrum gegangen. Peter hat gesagt, dass es ein neues Restaurant gibt. Aber wir haben es nicht gesehen.

Nuts and bolts

1 Back to the past – and a bit of bad news … Remember when Claire said: **Wir sind in ein Café gegangen.** *We have gone/we went into a café.* She actually said: *we **are** gone into a café.*

When you talk about something that involves movement to or from a place, like **gehen** go, **fahren** go (by transport)/drive or **fliegen** fly you use **ich bin**, **Sie sind**, **er/sie/es ist**, **wir sind** and **sie sind** plus the special form of the 'action' word, the one that describes what you did. So you are really saying… I am gone or I am flown.

You also do this with the verb **sein** be. For example: I have been becomes I **am** been: **Ich bin gewesen**.

Here are four more examples:

ich bin gegangen *I have gone/I went*
Sie sind gefahren *you have gone (by transport)/you went*
er ist geflogen *he has flown/he flew*
wir sind gewesen *we have been/we were*

2 And another bit of bad news:

… **dass** er nach Frankfurt **fliegt** … *that he flies to Frankfurt*
… **dass** er ein Auto **gesehen hat** … *that he has seen a car*

Watch out when you see **dass** (that) – because:

- the verb rushes to the end: … **dass** er nach Frankfurt **fliegt**
- if you are talking about the past, the auxiliary verb (the one meaning *have*), goes *right* to the end: … **dass** er ein Auto gesehen **hat**.

If all this is getting too complicated stop right here! Listen to it on the **recording** and then try the exercise in **Let's speak German!** You'll realise it's not that difficult.

3 **er**, **sie**, **es**   *it*

Now here's another hole to fall into: You learnt that: **er**, **sie**, **es** means *he*, *she*, *it*. If we wanted to talk about **der Mann**, **die Frau** or **das Kind** (the child) we could say: Der Mann ist hier. **Er** ist hier. Die Frau ist gross. **Sie** ist gross. Das Kind ist klein. **Es** ist klein. Just as we do in English. But what happens when you talk about *things*, like: **der** Mercedes, **die** Fahrkarte or **das** Haus? In English these are all **it**. In German they are referred to as **er**, **sie** or **es**, depending if the word is preceded by **der**, **die** or **das**:

Der Mercedes ist hier. **Er** ist hier. **Die** Fahrkarte ist teuer. **Sie** ist teuer. **Das** Haus ist billig. **Es** ist billig.

If you speak about more than one person or thing it's always **sie** (they):

Die Fahrkarten sind billig. **Sie** sind billig.

Let's speak German!

1 Practise the past using **gewesen**, **gekauft**, **gefahren**, **gesehen**, **gesagt**.

Say these sentences in German:

- Have you been to (in) Innsbruck in March?
- We went from Hannover to Braunschweig.
- Did he fly with Ryan Air from Stansted to Lübeck?
- I went from the supermarket to the hotel.
- He said that he has a car in England.
- I have seen lots of people in (on) the train to Vienna (Wien).
- Did you see that he drives a (einen) Ferrari?
- They said that they have seen the Black Forest.

2 **er**, **sie**, **es**

Decide if the word in brackets is **der**, **die** or **das**. Then complete the sentence with **er**, **sie** or **es**.

Example: *(the snow)* **Er** ist grau.

Now it's your turn:

(the car)	... **ist beim Supermarkt.**
(the bill)	... **ist gross.**
(the coffee)	... **ist schrecklich.**
(the people)	... **sind interessant.**
(the train)	... **fährt nicht nach Lübeck.**

3 Here are some prices. They are all in euros. For example:

€6,10: sechs Euro (und) zehn (Cents), €15.50: fünfzehn Euro (und) fünfzig (Cents)

Most Germans will leave out the words in brackets and will simply say: **sechs Euro zehn** and **fünfzehn Euro fünfzig**.

Now over to you. Say these prices in German:

€30,20   €6,35   €10,46   €72,50

Day 3

What to do today

An easy day!

- ✓ Read the five **New words**
- ✓ Read and work out the **Story** and the **New sentences**
- ✓ Read the **Nuts and bolts**
- ✓ Listen and speak along with the **recording**
- ✓ Learn today's five **New words** and the **New sentences** by heart
- ✓ **Let's speak German!** Only one exercise today
- ✓ Check your progress with the **recording**

The story

| Paul | **Warum gehen wir nicht mit Tom und Kate essen? Wir können in eine Pizzeria gehen oder besser – in ein nettes Restaurant. Haben sie ein Handy?** |
| Claire | **Ja, ich rufe sie an.** |

Today's new words

warum	*why*
essen gehen	*'eat go'/to go and eat*
besser	*better*
nett	*nice, pleasant*
sie	*they, them*

Today's new sentences

Warum gibt es hier keine Pizzeria? Ich möchte essen gehen. Das Restaurant ist besser. Die Leute sind sehr nett. Wir können sie auf dem Handy anrufen.

Let's speak German!

Practise **warum** and **denn**.

Make up the missing sentence, starting either with **warum** or **denn**. Like this:

> Warum möchten Sie ein neues Auto?
> Ich möchte ein neues Auto, **denn** mein Auto ist kaputt.

Now it's your turn:

- Warum kaufen Sie das Auto nicht? _____.
- _____ denn ich fahre nach Hamburg.
- _____ denn wir wollen essen gehen.
- Warum trinken Sie keinen Wein? _____.
- Warum wollen Sie das Schlosshotel anrufen? _____.
- _____ denn ich habe kein Geld.

Day 4

What to do today

✓ Read the five **New words**
✓ Read and work out the **Story** and the **New sentences**
✓ Look at the **Traveller's companion**. On pages 11 and 12 you'll find some useful words about **eating and drinking**
✓ Listen and speak along with the **recording**
✓ Learn today's five **New words** and the **New sentences** by heart
✓ Read about **gern** in the **Nuts and bolts**
✓ **Let's speak German!** You are going to take charge in the restaurant!
✓ Check your progress with the **recording**

The story

(In the restaurant)

Paul	**Was essen wir?**
Kate	**Ich nehme den Hackbraten und zu trinken – ein Mineralwasser.**
Tom	**Dasselbe für mich bitte, und ein Glas Wein.**
Claire	**Ich esse gern Spaghetti und zu trinken – ein Bier.**
Paul	**Ich nehme die Bratwurst und auch ein Bier.**

Today's new words

der Hackbraten	*the meatloaf*
trinken	*to drink*
das Mineralwasser	*the mineral water*
dasselbe	*the same*
gern	*with pleasure, to like doing something*

Today's new sentences

Zu essen?– Ich esse gern Bratwurst. Zu trinken? – Ich trinke gern Bier. Dasselbe für mich. Und ein Mineralwasser, bitte.

Nuts and bolts

gern

By adding this little word to the action word, you'll tell people that you *like* doing something:

> **Ich fliege gern**. I like flying. **Ich fahre gern nach München und ich gehe gern zum Hofbräuhaus.** I like driving to Munich, and I like going to the Hofbräuhaus.

Let's speak German!

1 Zu essen? Zu trinken?

Pretend you are having dinner with friends in a restaurant. You have to order for every one of the four people at your table. Use the words you have learned plus some of the ones in the **Traveller's companion** on pages 11 and 12. Here's an example:

> Den Hackbraten bitte, mit Rotkohl und Kartoffeln, und zu trinken ein Glas Rotwein, bitte.

Now order for your three friends in the same way. First the food and then **und zu trinken** … You can have the **Traveller's companion** open to help you along.

2 Memory test

I have picked four **New words** from every week you have done so far – that's a total of 20. Let's see how many you can remember. Say the words out loud and then check them yourself.

> but, how, broken, the snow, perhaps, two hours, the bill, on the right, my, a question, good, also, to see, a night, cash, now, better, that, more, why?

3 Gern

Make up five sentences, telling people what you like doing by adding **gern** to the action word.

Day 5

What to do today

✓ Read the five **New words**
✓ Read and work out the **Story** and the **New sentences**
✓ Listen and speak along with the **recording**
✓ Learn today's five **New words** and the **New sentences** by heart
✓ **Let's speak German!** Just one short exercise today
✓ Check your progress with the **recording**

The story

Die Kellnerin	Hier ist die Rechnung.
Tom	Die Rechnung ist für mich.
Paul	Nein, nein, bitte, das ist meine Rechnung. Claire, wo ist meine Kreditkarte? Sie ist weg.
Claire	Ich glaube, sie ist zu Hause.
Paul	Das ist schrecklich. Es tut mir leid, Tom. Ich habe keine Kreditkarte und kein Bargeld. Nur drei Euro.

Today's new words

weg, er/sie/es ist weg	*gone, it's gone*
ich glaube	*I think, I believe*
zu Hause	*at home*
schrecklich	*terrible*
nur	*only*

Today's new sentences

Mein Geld ist weg. Das ist schrecklich! Ist es nicht zu Hause? Nein, zu Hause habe ich nur sechs Euro. Ich glaube, es war mein Freund. Er ist auch weg.

Let's speak German!

Make up five sentences using the words in brackets. Start every sentence with: **Ich glaube** … and then again with: **Ich glaube**, dass … Just for some mental acrobatics moving action words about.

- Ich glaube, (schrecklich, Wein, Restaurant)
- Ich glaube, (ist, Deutschland, August, gefahren)
- Ich glaube, (wir haben, Kreditkarte, nur, es, gekauft)
- Ich glaube, (gesehen, Supermarkt, haben, rechts)
- Ich glaube, (zu Hause, weg)

Day 6

What to do today

✓ Read the five **New words**
✓ Read and work out the **Story** and the **New sentences**
✓ Look at the **Traveller's companion**. On pages 13, 14 and 15 you'll find some interesting **sample menus** for breakfast, lunch and dinner
✓ Listen and speak along with the **recording**
✓ Learn today's five **New words** and the **New sentences** by heart
✓ **Let's speak German!** More speaking practice for you
✓ Check your progress with the **recording**

The story

Tom	**Paul, bitte, es ist keine grosse Rechnung. Wo ist die Kellnerin? Sie hat meine Kreditkarte.**
Die Kellnerin	**Ich habe ein Problem: Die Kreditkarte ist kaputt.**
Tom	**Was ist los? Ein Problem? Das ist nicht möglich. Können sie bitte langsamer sprechen?**
Die Kellnerin	**Die – Kredit – karte – ist – kaputt.**

Today's new words

gross	*big*
der Kellner, die Kellnerin	*the waiter, the waitress*
Was ist los?	*What is the matter?*
Das ist nicht möglich.	*That isn't possible.*
Können Sie bitte langsamer sprechen?	*Can you speak more slowly, please?*

Today's new sentences

Was ist los? Ich rufe von London an. Könnnen Sie bitte langsamer sprechen? Sie haben ein grosses Problem? Das ist nicht möglich.

Let's speak German!

1 Warm up with the five **Flash sentences** for this week. Did you 'turn and learn'? Test yourself – speaking out loud – until you are word-perfect.

2 Something has happened. Something is wrong. You don't know what, so you ask: **Was ist los?**

Here's what happened – for you to say in German. Ask first *What's the matter?* and then reply.

- The restaurant is terrible. They don't have wine, only beer.
- I have not seen the bus, and I have to go to an appointment.
- My mobile phone is broken. Can you speak more slowly, please?
- I have a problem: The bill is large and I do not have a credit card.
- I think this is not possible: ten euros for a glass of wine?

3 Now for more food and drink …

Pretend you are out with your partner, for breakfast, lunch and dinner. After consulting the **Traveller's companion** (pages 13, 14 and 15), order two breakfasts, two lunches and two dinners. Place your orders speaking OUT LOUD! We can't check what you are saying, so don't skip it – we'll find out!

Day 7

Today you receive your reward for all the learning you've done during this week: a great result on your **Progress chart!** But first there's a little work to be done …

What to do today

✓ Read the whole **Story** out loud
✓ Do the speaking exercises which follow the **Story** and score up to 100%!

Here's this week's whole story …

Claire	**Paul, hier ist etwas sehr interessantes: Ich war im Supermarkt um Wein zu kaufen. Und ich habe zwei Freunde von London gesehen – Tom und Kate! Wir sind in ein Café gegangen, und Tom hat gesagt, dass er ein schönes Auto gesehen hat. Aber Kate will es nicht. Es ist sehr teuer.**
Paul	**Warum gehen wir nicht mit Tom und Kate essen? Wir können in eine Pizzeria gehen oder besser – in ein nettes Restaurant. Haben sie ein Handy?**
Claire	**Ja, ich rufe sie an.**

(In the restaurant)

Paul	**Was essen wir?**
Kate	**Ich nehme den Hackbraten und zu trinken – ein Mineralwasser.**
Tom	**Dasselbe für mich bitte, und ein Glas Wein.**
Claire	**Ich esse gern Spaghetti und zu trinken – ein Bier.**
Paul	**Ich nehme die Bratwurst und auch ein Bier.**
Die Kellnerin	**Hier ist die Rechnung.**
Tom	**Die Rechnung ist für mich.**
Paul	**Nein, nein, bitte, das ist meine Rechnung. Claire, wo ist meine Kreditkarte. Sie ist weg.**
Claire	**Ich glaube, sie ist zu Hause.**
Paul	**Das ist schrecklich. Es tut mir leid, Tom. Ich habe keine Kreditkarte und kein Bargeld. Nur drei Euro.**
Tom	**Paul, bitte, es ist keine grosse Rechnung. Wo ist die Kellnerin? Sie hat meine Kreditkarte.**

Die Kellnerin	Ich habe ein Problem: Die Kreditkarte ist kaputt.
Tom	Was ist los? Ein Problem? Das ist nicht möglich. Können sie bitte langsamer sprechen?
Die Kellnerin	Die – Kredit – karte – ist – kaputt.

Tell me, tell me – in the past!

… that you went to the supermarket today, that you saw a lot of people in the supermarket, that you bought water, beer and wine, that you went by car and that you saw Anna, a friend … that Anna saw your car at the cafeteria of the supermarket … that she said: 'I'd like to go and eat a pizza' … and that you went into a restaurant… that the bill was very large and that Anna said 'Oh, good grief' and that after (nach) two bottles of wine you called a taxi, and you were home by 12 pm.

When you have 'told me', listen to the German on the recording. Give yourself between 10 and 25 points depending on how well you did.

Remember your words?

- Take out all the **Flash cards** for Weeks 3 and 4 – 30 for each week. Out of each 30 pick 15 at random.
- With the English facing you test yourself, saying the German out loud. Check after each word.
- Put the correct cards to one side and the ones you got wrong or did not know to the other. Give yourself a point for each one you got right.
- Have a quick look at the ones you did not know. Spend five minutes on these.

Remember the story?

Answer these questions in German – OUT LOUD – and in full sentences.

- Wo ist Claire gewesen?
- Warum war sie im Supermarkt?
- Wo war sie mit Tom und Kate?
- Was hat Tom gesagt?
- Warum will Kate das Auto nicht kaufen?
- Wo haben die vier Freunde gegessen?
- Was möchte Claire essen?

- Was möchte Tom trinken?
- Was ist schrecklich?
- Hat die Kellnerin ein Problem? Warum?

If you struggled through this exercise give yourself 10 points, if you marched through it make it 20. And if you raced through it give yourself 25 points.

From the Traveller's companion …

- Say 10 numbers between 11 and 50.
- Give 10 items you may find on a menu.

After you have said them write them down and check them in the **Traveller's companion**. Score up to 20 points.

Your result this week

✓ Tell me, tell me …	/25
✓ Remember your words?	/30
✓ Remember the story?	/25
✓ From the Traveller's companion	/20

Total score /100% **Date** _____

Depending on your score you can either pat yourself on the back, wring your hands or … do it again!

Don't forget to enter your result on the **Progress chart**.

week

06

ich brauche einen Arzt

I need a doctor

The story continues …

Paul is not feeling well. Too much Bratwurst and Sauerkraut? Too much Weisswein and Bier? Claire phones for a medical appointment. When they arrive late at the surgery and find out that they've missed the doctor, Paul makes a remarkable recovery …

Day 1

What to do today

✓ Read the five **New words**

✓ **About time!** This is a chapter in the **Traveller's companion**. Have a first look at it – it's on page 18. You'll practise it tomorrow. Then turn to page 23 for the essential verb **wissen**

✓ Read and work out the **Story** and the **New sentences**

✓ Listen to and speak along with the **recording**

✓ Learn today's five **New words** and the **New sentences** by heart

✓ Test yourself with **Let's speak German!**

✓ Check your progress with the **recording**

The story

Paul   **Ich brauche einen Arzt. Ich kann nicht essen. Ich kann nicht trinken, nur Tee. Ich weiss nicht, was los ist.**

Claire   **Oh. Es tut mir leid. Ja, wir brauchen einen Arzt.** *(on the phone)* **Hallo, guten Tag, ich möchte einen Termin mit dem Arzt ... Ja, ich warte ... Ja, für heute ... Um wieviel Uhr? ... Gut. Ja, danke. Der Name? Blair. B–l–a–i–r. Ja, wie Tony.**

Today's new words

Ich weiss nicht	*I don't know*
der Arzt	*the doctor*
ich warte	*I wait*
um wieviel Uhr	*at what time?*
wie	*like, how*

Today's new sentences

Um wieviel Uhr haben Sie einen Termin? Ich weiss nicht. Ich glaube es war um drei. Und Ihr Name? Thatcher, ja, wie Margaret.

Let's speak German!

1 ich weiss es, **ich weiss es nicht – ich weiss/ich weiss nicht**, **dass/wo/wann/wer…**

Remember to move the action word to the end of the sentence after ich weiss/ich weiss nicht, **dass**, **wo**, **wann** etc.

Say these sentences in German:

- What does he want to eat? I know it.
- I am sorry, I don't know it.
- I know that they have a house in Manchester.
- I don't know where the supermarket is.
- I don't know when the train goes to Berlin.
- I know who would like the Ferrari.
- I don't know how much the appointment with the doctor costs.
- I don't know why she has a problem.

2 Speak OUT LOUD – and complete these sentences:

- Wo ist der Arzt? Ich weiss es nicht. Ich glaube, er …
- Um wieviel Uhr ist der Termin? Ich weiss nicht, aber ich glaube …
- Wann haben Sie Urlaub? Ich weiss es nicht, vielleicht …
- Ist Manchester gross? So wie München? Ich weiss es nicht, aber ich glaube, dass …
- Ich trinke gern Tee, aber heute …

Day 2

What to do today

✓ Read the five **New words**
✓ Read and work out the **Story** and the **New sentences**
✓ Listen to and speak along with the **recording**
✓ Take another look at **About time!** in the **Traveller's companion**
✓ Learn today's five **New words** and the **New sentences** by heart
✓ **Let's speak German!** Two easy speaking exercises for you
✓ Check your progress with the **recording**

The story

Claire Wir haben einen Termin beim Arzt. Um halb drei. Es ist jetzt elf.
Paul Ich möchte zu den Geschäften, und ich brauche eine Bank.
Claire Wir haben vier Stunden für alles. Das ist genug.

Today's new words

halb drei	*half past two, 'half two'**
die Geschäfte	*the shops*
die Bank	*the bank*
alles	*all*
genug	*enough*

*Beware of the confusion: Germans say '**halb zwei**' which may sound like 'half two', i.e. half *past* two. But **halb zwei** is 'half *towards* the two', i.e. half *past* one.

Today's new sentences

Ich brauche keine Geschäfte. Ich habe alles. Aber nicht genug Geld. Gibt es hier eine Bank?

Let's speak German!

1 Complete these questions to fit the answers:

- Wann … ?   *Answer*: Ich muss um neun Uhr zu den Geschäften.
- Warum … ?   *Answer*: Denn die Restaurants sind teuer.
- Wieviel kosten … ?   *Answer*: Die sechs Glas Bier kosten achtzehn Euro.
- Was … ?   *Answer*: Ich will alles kaufen … ehm … ich möchte eine Flasche Wasser kaufen.
- Haben Sie … ?   *Answer*: Ja, wir haben genug von Bonn gesehen.

2 Telling the time: Had a good look at the **Traveller's companion**? In that case say in German:

- What time is it? At what time are we going?
- It is half past three. We are flying at half past three.
- It is five o' clock. We are in Köln at five o'clock.
- It is a quarter to nine in the evening (am Abend). We are driving to Berlin at 20.45.
- It is a quarter past seven. We are going at a quarter past seven.
- It is one o'clock. We are eating at one o' clock.

Day 3

What to do today
✓ Read the five **New words**
✓ Read and work out the **Story** and the **New sentences**
✓ Read the **Nuts and bolts**
✓ Take out the **Traveller's companion**. On page 28 you'll find some **everyday adjectives**. Have a read through
✓ Listen to and speak along with the **recording**
✓ Learn today's five **New words** and the **New sentences** by heart
✓ **Let's speak German!** Two easy speaking exercises
✓ Check your progress with the **recording**

The story
Claire Es gibt eine Bank und Geschäfte nicht weit von der Hauptstrasse.
Paul Ich suche etwas für das Auto von Helmut. Ich glaube die Geschäfte sind billiger hier. Wann ist die Bank offen?

Today's new words
nicht weit von	*not far from*
die Hauptstrasse	*the main road*
etwas	*something, also: a little*
billiger	*cheaper*
offen	*open*

Today's new sentences
Gibt es Geschäfte nicht weit von hier? Sind sie billiger? Ich brauche etwas für meine Frau. Wann ist die Bank offen?

Nuts and bolts
If you want to say *cheaper, nicer, smaller* or *more interesting* in German this is very easy. Most of the time you add **-er**, just like in English.

So it's: **billiger**, **netter**, **kleiner** or **interessanter**.
Occasionally the two dots (the Umlaut) appear, and **gross** becomes **grösser**, or **kalt** (cold) becomes **kälter**. But it's all quite easy.

Let's speak German!

1 Say these sentences in German. They include ten everyday adjectives from the **Traveller's companion**. Take another look at page 28 to help you.

- It is difficult to do everything: First I must go to the doctor's and at eleven …
- It is an old house and always dirty.
- It is a fast car and dangerous.
- Maria is likeable and very kind.
- It is mad to drink ten glasses of wine but it is not forbidden.

2 etwas: to say *something new* or *something old* you add **-es** to the adjective. So it's **etwas neues**, **etwas altes**.

Now you say: something beautiful, something interesting, something hot, something cheap, something cold.

etwas can also mean *a little*, like: *a little big* or *a little bigger* **etwas gross**, **etwas grösser**.

Over to you, say these sentences in German:

- The shoes are a little small; I would like them a little bigger.
- The Schnitzel is a little cold; I would like it a little warmer.
- The question is a little difficult; I would like it a little easier.

Day 4

What to do today

✓ Read the five **New words**
✓ Read and work out the **Story** and the **New sentences**
✓ **I am ill!** Consult page 10 of the **Traveller's companion** to get help. Have a read through
✓ Listen to and speak along with the **recording**
✓ Learn today's five **New words** and the **New sentences** by heart
✓ **Let's speak German!** Two easy speaking exercises
✓ Check your progress with the **recording**

The story

Claire Aber das Auto ist in Ordnung. Helmut hat die ganze Nacht an dem Auto gearbeitet.

Paul Ja, aber es ist kein neues Auto. Es ist alt und schrecklich.

Today's new words

in Ordnung	*ok, all right*
ganz, die ganze Nacht	*whole, the whole night*
an	*at*
hat gearbeitet	*has worked*
alt	*old*

Today's new sentences

Ich habe die ganze Nacht gearbeitet. Das ist nicht in Ordnung. Aber ich bin alt und habe kein Geld.

Let's speak German!

1 Say these sentences in German – OUT LOUD:

- The car is old and it's cheap but it's not ok.
- They are at home but not the whole night.
- I have seen you at the restaurant with Helmut and Karin.
- Is it all right if I eat everything?
- Did he work or didn't he work? I don't know.

2 Doctor, **doctor** … Complete these sentences by giving the German for the English words in brackets.

- Ich möchte etwas für _____. (*stomach pains*)
- Ich habe _____. (*a backache*)
- Ich muss zur _____. (*chemist's*)
- Haben Sie etwas gegen _____? (*a headache*)
- Ich habe _____ (*the tablets*) und jetzt brauche ich _____. (*an invoice and a receipt*)

Day 5

What to do today

✓ Read the five **New words**
✓ Read and work out the **Story** and the **New sentences**
✓ More numbers: they are on page 16 in the **Traveller's companion**. Have a look at numbers **50 to 1,000**
✓ Listen to and speak along with the **recording**
✓ Learn today's five **New words** and the **New sentences** by heart
✓ **Let's speak German!** Two easy speaking exercises
✓ Check your progress with the **recording**

The story

(Later)

Claire **Wir haben viele Sachen gekauft, und ein neues Handy. Paul, wir haben jetzt fünf Handys!**

Paul **Das Handy war billig, es kostet weniger hier – viel mehr in England. Aber jetzt müssen wir zum Arzt. Wo wohnt er?**

Claire **Ich glaube in der Mozart Strasse.**

Paul **Ah, hier, Nummer zwölf.**

Today's new words

die Sache, Sachen	*the thing, things*
weniger	*less*
mehr	*more*
wohnen, wohnt	*to live, lives*
die Nummer	*the number*

Today's new sentences

Wir wohnen jetzt weit entfernt vom Zentrum. Beethoven Strasse Nummer 10. Wir haben mehr Sachen aber weniger Freunde.

Let's speak German!

1 Use the action words in their correct form and join all the words to make a sentence.

- Fahrkarten – denn – kaufen – müssen – ich – wir – sein – sechs – viele
- weniger – Helmut – haben – möchten – essen – denn – Magenschmerzen – er
- Sie – wohnen – in der – Strasse – wo – sieben? – Nummer?
- zu Hause – meine – denn – Sachen – nicht – brauchen – sein – ich – sie

2 More number practice.

Say these numbers in German. You can use the **Traveller's companion** to help you. Say the numbers twice with help, and then try once more without looking.

66, 75, 97, 350, 500, 620, 844, 100

Day 6

What to do today

✓ Read the five **New words**
✓ Read and work out the **Story** and the **New sentences**
✓ Listen to and speak along with the **recording**
✓ Learn today's five **New words** and the **New sentences** by heart
✓ **Let's speak German!** One quick exercise and one that's a little longer …
✓ Check your progress with the **recording**

The story

(At the surgery)

Paul Guten Tag, mein Name ist Blair. Ich habe einen Termin um halb drei.

Ursula Es tut mir leid, aber der Termin war um halb zwei. Sie sind zu spät. Der Arzt ist nach Hause gegangen. Wir haben jetzt geschlossen.

(In the car)

Claire Und jetzt? Was machen wir jetzt?

Paul Nichts. Es macht nichts. Mit dem neuen Handy brauche ich keinen Arzt. Wir gehen jetzt essen. Vielleicht einen Schweinebraten oder Heringssalat.

Today's new words

zu	*too*
spät	*late*
nach Hause	*home*
geschlossen	*closed*
nichts	*nothing*

Today's new sentences

Wir sind zu spät zum Restaurant gegangen. Es war geschlossen. Wir haben nichts gegessen und sind nach Hause gegangen.

Let's speak German!

1 Speed test: Say these sentences *really quickly* in German. Try 20 seconds.

Where is the number? The shop is closed. The tea is too hot. The bus is too late. I have nothing. The things are old. We want more, not less. Where do you live? It's gone, it doesn't matter.

2 You've been offered these appointments. Say them out loud in German:

Here's an example:

Tuesday 11 March at 3 o'clock. **Dienstag, der elfte März um 3 Uhr**.

Note: **-te** after **elf**. This is the way *the eleventh* is translated. **zwanzig – der zwanzigste**. **fünf – der fünfte**.

Remember: am: **morgens**, pm: **abends**, **nachts**.

Now you try:

- Monday 12 June at 10 am
- 22 August at 7 pm
- Thursday 3 October at 11 pm
- Friday 20 December at 8.30 am
- 30 March at 6 am
- Sunday 14 May at 14.45

If it took you a long time to work them out say them again … in half the time!

Day 7

It's the end of the week! Only one more week to go. Meanwhile let's start on the self-assessment.

What to do today

✓ Read the whole **Story** out loud
✓ Then complete the five exercises which follow and score maximum points

Here's this week's whole story ...

Paul	**Ich brauche einen Arzt. Ich kann nicht essen. Ich kann nicht trinken, nur Tee. Ich weiss nicht, was los ist.**
Claire	**Oh. Es tut mir leid. Ja, wir brauchen einen Arzt.** *(on the phone)* **Hallo, guten Tag, ich möchte einen Termin mit dem Arzt. ... Ja, ich warte ... Ja, für heute ... Um wieviel Uhr? ... Gut. Ja, danke. Der Name? Blair. B–l–a–i–r. Ja, wie Tony.**
	(later) **Wir haben einen Termin beim Arzt. Um halb drei. Es ist jetzt elf.**
Paul	**Ich möchte zu den Geschäften, und ich brauche eine Bank.**
Claire	**Wir haben vier Stunden für alles. Das ist genug. Es gibt eine Bank und Geschäfte nicht weit von der Hauptstrasse.**
Paul	**Ich suche etwas für das Auto von Helmut. Ich glaube die Geschäfte sind billiger hier. Wann ist die Bank offen?**
Claire	**Aber das Auto ist in Ordnung. Helmut hat die ganze Nacht an dem Auto gearbeitet.**
Paul	**Ja, aber es ist kein neues Auto. Es ist alt und schrecklich.**
(Later)	
Claire	**Wir haben viele Sachen gekauft, und ein neues Handy. Paul, wir haben jetzt fünf Handys!**
Paul	**Das Handy war billig, es kostet weniger hier – viel mehr in England. Aber jetzt müssen wir zum Arzt. Wo wohnt er?**
Claire	**Ich glaube in der Mozart Strasse.**
Paul	**Ah, hier, Nummer zwölf.**

(At the surgery)

Paul Guten Tag, mein Name ist Blair. Ich habe einen Termin um halb drei.

Ursula Es tut mir leid, aber der Termin war um halb zwei. Sie sind zu spät. Der Arzt ist nach Hause gegangen. Wir haben jetzt geschlossen.

(In the car)

Claire Und jetzt? Was machen wir jetzt?

Paul Nichts. Es macht nichts. Mit dem neuen Handy brauche ich keinen Arzt. Wir gehen jetzt essen. Vielleicht einen Schweinebraten oder Heringssalat.

Tell me, tell me ...

... that you have a stomachache, that you do not like it and that you have to go to the doctor's ... that your friend said there is a good doctor and that he is in the centre of Munich near the main road in the Wagner Strasse, number 54 ... that you have an appointment today at 9 o'clock in the morning.

... that you have been to the doctor and that he was very kind, and that he said it was nothing, only too much beer and Currywurst ... that the bill was not large – only 30 euros – and that you went to a restaurant for a Schnitzel and a small glass of white wine.

When you have said the piece OUT LOUD and listened to it on the **recording** give yourself 10 points for a fair attempt, 20 for quite good and 25 points for very good.

Remember in a flash

Take out the **Flash sentences** from Weeks 2, 3 and 4, a total of 16 cards. With the English facing you say the German and then check. If you can say all of the sentences in a flash give yourself full marks – 30 points. If it takes a little longer or you don't get it quite right give yourself half marks for each sentence.

At the pharmacy

You are planning a weekend in the Alps and are stocking up at the pharmacy – just in case.

- Say you would like something for a headache.
- Ask them if they have something for a stomachache.
- Tell them you need a cream for your back.
- Tell them you have a cough, but only at night. Do they have a linctus?
- Tell them you need an invoice and a receipt.
- Ask them how much it is.
- Tell them that you are sorry but that you do not have cash.
- Ask them if a credit card is ok.
- Ask them if there is a doctor nearby.
- Say goodbye and thank them for everything.

After saying it all OUT LOUD listen to the **recording** and give yourself between five and 15 points, depending on how well you did.

Bonus adjectives

Have another five-minute read of the everyday 'bonus' adjectives on page 28 of the **Traveller's companion**. Read them OUT LOUD to yourself three or four times. Now close the booklet. How many of them can you remember and use to describe each of the words below? Here's an example:

das Haus – das Haus ist **sauber**

If you cannot think of a bonus adjective use one of the familiar ones or even a colour.

das Auto, das Geschäft, die Sachen, die Nummer, die Strasse, der Tee, das Hotel, der Kellner, die Flasche, die Leute

A bonus adjective earns you two points, any adjective or colour you learned already earns you one point.

Remember your verbs

Just to make sure your verbs don't get rusty, here are ten to remember. Say these phrases in German and give yourself one point for each correct one.

he has worked, I have seen, she wants to drink, he cannot eat, I cannot go, she has gone, they buy, you go shopping, I would like to call, we are looking for …

Your result this week

✓ Tell me, tell me …   /25

✓ Remember in a flash   /30

✓ At the pharmacy   /15

✓ Bonus adjectives   /20

✓ Remember your verbs   /10

Total score   **/100%**   **Date** _____

A great result? Record it on the **Progress chart!**

07

auf Wiedersehen München – aber wir haben die Fotos!

good bye Munich – but we have the photos!

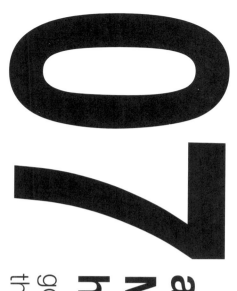

The story concludes …

It's the end of their holiday with a last-minute rush buying presents and taking photos. Then it's off to the airport in Helmut's unreliable car. Will Paul and Claire miss the plane? Will they argue over the photos? And what does Paul have up his sleeve?

Day 1

What to do today

✓ Read the five **New words**
✓ Read and work out the **Story** and the **New sentences**
✓ Take a final look at the **Traveller's companion**. There are some **useful verbs** for 'the inspired' on page 27 which will come in handy. Browse through them …
✓ Listen to and speak along with the **recording**
✓ Learn today's five **New words** and the **New sentences** by heart
✓ **Let's speak German!** Two easy speaking exercises …
✓ Check your progress with the **recording**

The story

Paul   Ich kann es nicht glauben. Es ist schon Samstag. Morgen fliegen wir leider nach England. Was machen wir heute?

Claire   Ich brauche ein Warenhaus. Ich muss etwas für meinen Chef kaufen. Das ist wichtig.

Today's new words

schon	*already*
leider	*unfortunately*
das Warenhaus	*the department store*
der Chef	*the boss, manager*
wichtig	*important*

Today's new sentences

Ich habe meinen Chef im Warenhaus gesehen. Was hat er gekauft? Ein Handy. Ich habe es schon gesehen. Morgen kaufe ich dasselbe.

Let's speak German!

1 machen – müssen – brauchen

Ask someone what he or she is doing – now, here, in a place, today. Then answer, using **müssen** and **brauchen**. For example:

Was **machen** Sie heute in Köln? Ich **muss** zu VW. Ich **brauche** etwas für meinen Golf.

Now you try:

* machen – müssen (Warenhaus) – brauchen (Mantel, Wetter)
* machen – müssen (Geldautomat) – brauchen (Bargeld, Rechnung)
* machen – müssen (Arzt) – brauchen (Tabletten, Schmerzen)
* machen – müssen (Supermarkt) – brauchen (Obst, etwas zu trinken)

2 A few extra verbs from the **Traveller's companion** … for 'the inspired'.

ankommen – angekommen arrive – arrived
sprechen – gesprochen speak – spoken
kommen – gekommen come – come
reparieren – repariert   repair – repaired

… and now eight easy sentences for you to say in German:

* They must arrive tomorrow.
* My boss arrived yesterday with his new car.
* He would like to speak English (Englisch).
* He did not speak English in Germany.
* We must come to the train with Helga.
* She has come with a terrible friend.
* Who can repair the car tomorrow?
* We have already repaired the car.

Day 2

What to do today

✓ Read the five **New words**
✓ Read and work out the **Story** and the **New sentences**
✓ Listen to and speak along with the **recording**
✓ Learn today's five **New words** and the **New sentences** by heart
✓ **Let's speak German!** Two easy speaking exercises
✓ Check your progress with the **recording**

The story

Paul   **Ich möchte Fotos machen. Wir haben kein Foto von uns. Wer kann uns helfen? Ist hier jemand… ?**

Claire   *(Turning to a stranger)* **Oh, entschuldigen Sie. Können Sie uns bitte helfen? Wir möchten ein Foto machen. Ja, mit meinem Mann, hier am Tisch.**

Today's new words

das Foto, die Fotos	*the photo, the photos*
uns	*us*
wer	*who*
mein Mann	*my husband*
der Tisch	*the table*

Today's new sentences

Kann uns jemand helfen? Wer kann ein Foto machen?
Mein Mann möchte ein Foto von uns am Tisch.

Let's speak German!

1 Make up five short sentences starting with these sentences openers:

- Die Fotos sind …
- Bei uns …
- Wer hat … ?
- Mein Mann möchte …
- Der Tisch ist …

2 It's the last round of mental acrobatics. Here are four more verbs for 'the inspired', then say the sentences below in German.

geben – gegeben	give – given
schreiben – geschrieben	write – written
hoffen – gehofft	hope – hoped
nehmen – genommen	take – taken

- She wants to give something to Frau Müller.
- He has given us a lot of money.
- I want to write to the director of Air Berlin.
- We hope that the weather is beautiful in May.
- I take the car but who has taken the cash?

Day 3

What to do today

✓ Read the five **New words**
✓ Read and work out the **Story** and the **New sentences**
✓ Listen to and speak along with the **recording**
✓ Learn today's five **New words** and the **New sentences** by heart
✓ **Let's speak German!** Two easy speaking exercises
✓ Check your progress with the **recording**

The story

Paul	**Es ist Sonntag. Auf Wiedersehen Deutschland! Schade. Das Wetter in England ist schlecht, und am Montag muss ich arbeiten.**
Elke	**Aber Birmingham ist interessant, ja?**
Helmut	**Hier ist mein Auto. Wir müssen zum Flughafen. Wir haben nicht viel Zeit.**

Today's new words

auf Wiedersehen	*Good bye*
Schade, wie schade!	*pity, What a pity!*
das Wetter	*the weather*
der Flughafen	*the airport*
die Zeit	*the time*

Today's new sentences

Wir sind im Flughafen, aber wir können nicht fliegen. Das Wetter ist schrecklich. Wie schade! Aber ich habe viel Zeit, um auf Wiedersehen zu sagen.

Let's speak German!

1 In the next three sentences you'll find all the 15 words you have learnt in the last three days. Finish off every sentence with **schade**! or **Wie schade**!

- Goodbye, the weather here is beautiful but my husband must (go) already tomorrow to England. What a pity!
- I don't have time for a photo of us at the table at the café in the airport. Pity!

- Who is the boss of the department store and what does he do? I want to work there but the store is always closed. Pity.

Warum – denn, weil
Remember? **denn** and **weil** both mean *because*. After **denn** the words which follow stay in the same order as in English. After **weil** the action word has to go to the end of the sentence. For example:

Wir können nicht fliegen, **denn** das Wetter **ist** schlecht.
Wir können nicht fliegen, **weil** das Wetter schlecht **ist**.

2 Now answer these questions first with **denn** and then with **weil**:

- Warum kaufen Sie kein neues Auto? Ich kaufe kein neues Auto, denn/weil …
- Warum muss Helmut zur Bank? Helmut muss zur Bank, denn/weil …
- Warum braucht Claire kein Bargeld? Claire braucht kein Bargeld, denn/weil …
- Warum rufen Sie den Flughafen an? Ich rufe den Flughafen an, denn/weil …
- Warum ist Gert zum Bus gegangen? Gert ist zum Bus gegangen, denn/weil …

Day 4

What to do today

✓ Read the five **New words**
✓ Read and work out the **Story** and the **New sentences**
✓ Listen to and speak along with the **recording**
✓ Learn today's five **New words** and the **New sentences** by heart
✓ **Let's speak German!** Only one easy bit of speaking practice today
✓ Check your progress with the **recording**

The story

(auf der Autobahn)

Helmut	**Es tut mir leid, aber wir haben ein Problem. Oh, meine Güte! Wir haben kein Benzin!**
Elke	**Hier ist eine Ausfahrt und da ist die Bushaltestelle. Und da ist der Bus!**
Paul	**Zwei zum Flughafen, bitte.**
Bus driver	**Hin und zurück?**
Paul	**Nein, nein, nur hin.**

Today's new words

die Autobahn	*the motorway*
das Benzin	*the petrol*
da	*there*
die Haltestelle	*the stop (for metros, buses and trains)*
hin und zurück	*'there and back', return*

Today's new sentences

Eine Fahrkarte hin und zurück: acht Euro. Das Benzin: zehn Euro. Die Bushaltestelle? Da, rechts, bei der Autobahn.

Let's speak German!

Have another look at the last two pieces of the **Story**, days 3 and 4. Then answer these questions in whole sentences, still speaking OUT LOUD!

Day 3
- Warum will Paul nicht nach England (gehen)?
- Wann muss er arbeiten?
- Wie ist das Wetter im April in Birmingham?
- Wie fahren sie zum Flughafen?

Day 4
- Warum hat Helmut ein Problem auf der Autobahn?
- Paul kauft keine vier Fahrkarten im Bus. Warum nicht?
- Kauft Paul Fahrkarten, für hin und zurück?
- Wo ist die Haltestelle für den Bus zum Flughafen?
- Was müssen Elke und Helmut mit dem Auto machen?

Day 5

What to do today

✓ Read the five **New words**
✓ Read and work out the **Story** and the **New sentences**
✓ Listen to and speak along with the **recording**
✓ Learn today's five **New words** and the **New sentences** by heart
✓ **Let's speak German!** Two easy speaking exercises
✓ Check your progress with the **recording**

The story

(Im Flugzeug)

Paul Wir haben gegessen. Was können wir jetzt machen? Gibt es eine Zeitung?

Claire Ich habe die Fotos!

Paul Ah, hier ist das Foto von dem BMW, und hier ist Tom, gestern im Hofbräuhaus, ohne Bier aber mit einer Flasche Wein.

Claire *Eine* Flasche? ... Gestern? Es war ein bisschen mehr, drei oder vier!

Today's new words

die Zeitung	*the newspaper*
gestern	*yesterday*
das Hofbräuhaus	*Hofbräuhaus (famous Munich beer garden)*
ohne	*without*
ein bisschen	*a little*

Today's new sentences

Ich bin in München ohne meine Freundin. Das Hofbräuhaus gefällt mir nicht. Das Bier ist ein bisschen teuer. Die Zeitung ist von gestern. Ich fahre weg.

Let's speak German!

1 Lets talk about today's **Story**. Answer these questions in German, in full sentences.

- Was sucht Paul im Flugzeug?
- Haben sie die Fotos gesehen?
- Wer ist Tom?
- Wo haben sie das Foto von Tom gemacht?
- Wieviel Flaschen Wein haben sie getrunken?

2 When you know your **New sentences** by heart give me these variations:

- I am in Frankfurt with my husband.
- The beer is a little warm.
- The newspaper comes from England. It is not from yesterday.
- We are going to Berlin, without a problem.
- I love the Hofbräuhaus in October.

Day 6

What to do today

✓ Read the five **New words**
✓ Read and work out the **Story** and the **New sentences**
✓ Listen to and speak along with the **recording**
✓ Learn today's five **New words** and the **New sentences** by heart
✓ **Let's speak German!** The last two easy speaking exercises
✓ Check your progress with the **recording**

The story

Paul	**Was ist los?**
Claire	**Die Fotos von München sind zu klein. Und warum drei Fotos von der Tankstelle? Und wer ist die Frau im Bikini?**
Paul	**Es tut mir leid. Ja, die Fotos sind schrecklich. Aber ich habe eine gute Idee! Nächstes Jahr fliegen wir an die Côte d'Azur. Ich habe einen Freund bei Air France. Er hat ein Haus in …**
Claire	**Also los!**

Today's new words

klein	*small*
die Tankstelle	*the petrol station*
die Idee	*the idea*
nächstes Jahr	*next year*
Also los! (colloqu.)	*Let´s go!*

Today's new sentences

Diese Tankstelle ist zu klein. Und sie hat kein Benzin. Das Auto ist immer ein Problem. Nächstes Jahr fahren wir nach Berlin mit dem Zug. Eine gute Idee!

Let's speak German!

1 Take out all of the **Flash sentences** from the last two weeks and test yourself – speaking OUT LOUD – until you are word-perfect.

2 Have another look at today's **Story**. Decide if these statements are right or wrong. Then respond to them in German, in whole sentences starting with **ja** or **nein**.

- Paul and Claire have eaten on the plane.
- Claire wants to see the photos.
- They only have a few photos.
- The photos of Munich are too small.
- Did Paul take two photos of the petrol station?
- Is there a photo of a woman in a bikini?
- Does Paul want to go to Mallorca next year?
- Do you think that Paul and Claire speak more German now?

Day 7

It's the last day of your course! Today you'll receive your **Certificate!** Today you could catch a plane to Munich and follow in the footsteps of Paul and Claire, speaking German – all the time! But first there's some work to be finished …

What to do today

✓ Before you start on the **Story** open the **Traveller's companion** on page 29. The Mini-dictionary shows all 210 words which you learned during the last seven weeks. Just in case you get stuck …

✓ Enjoy reading the final complete **Story** out loud. It's the longest one ever. There are over 250 words, and you know them all!

✓ Work through the final exercises which follow

✓ Add up your points for this week and then calculate your overall course result

✓ Fill in your **Certificate**. It will spell out how well you have done

Congratulations! Herzlichen Glückwunsch!

Here's this week's whole story

Paul	Ich kann es nicht glauben. Es ist schon Samstag. Morgen fliegen wir leider nach England. Was machen wir heute?
Claire	Ich brauche ein Warenhaus. Ich muss etwas für meinen Chef kaufen. Das ist wichtig.
Paul	Ich möchte Fotos machen. Wir haben kein Foto von uns. Wer kann uns helfen? Ist hier jemand … ?
Claire	*(Turning to a stranger)* Oh, entschuldigen Sie. Können Sie uns bitte helfen? Wir möchten ein Foto machen. Ja, mit meinem Mann, hier am Tisch.
Paul	Es ist Sonntag. Auf Wiedersehen Deutschland! Schade. Das Wetter in England ist schlecht, und am Montag muss ich arbeiten.
Elke	Aber Birmingham ist interessant, ja?
Helmut	Hier ist mein Auto. Wir müssen zum Flughafen. Wir haben nicht viel Zeit.

(auf der Autobahn)

Helmut	Es tut mir leid, aber wir haben ein Problem. Oh, meine Güte! Wir haben kein Benzin!
Elke	Hier ist eine Ausfahrt und da ist die Bushaltestelle. Und da ist der Bus!
Paul	Zwei zum Flughafen, bitte.
Bus driver	Hin und zurück?
Paul	Nein, nein, nur hin.

(Im Flugzeug)

Paul	Wir haben gegessen. Was können wir jetzt machen? Gibt es eine Zeitung?
Claire	Ich habe die Fotos!
Paul	Ah, hier ist das Foto von dem BMW, und hier ist Tom, gestern im Hofbräuhaus, ohne Bier aber mit einer Flasche Wein.
Claire	*Eine* Flasche? ... Gestern? Es war ein bisschen mehr, drei oder vier!
Paul	Was ist los?
Claire	Die Fotos von München sind zu klein. Und warum drei Fotos von der Tankstelle? Und wer ist die Frau im Bikini?
Paul	Es tut mir leid. Ja, die Fotos sind schrecklich. Aber ich habe eine gute Idee! Nächstes Jahr fliegen wir an die Côte d'Azur. Ich habe einen Freund bei Air France. Er hat ein Haus in ...
Claire	Also los!

And now for the final test on your progress!

Last word check

Take out the 60 **Flash cards** from weeks 3 and 4. Do you still remember the words which you learned some time ago? Spread them out with the English facing you. Close your eyes and pick 20 cards at random. Now give the German for each one. Score a maximum of 20 points.

Do the next four exercises with your tutor on the **recording** and with a pen in your hand to write down your score.

Tell me, tell me….

Can you remember what happened? (Have a quick look at the **Story** if you can't.) Answer these questions in German – and of course – OUT LOUD! Give yourself three points for each question which you answered easily, two points if you had to struggle a bit and one point for a good attempt.

- Wann müssen Paul und Claire nach England fliegen?
- Was will Claire am Samstag machen?
- Was will Paul am Samstag machen?
- Kann jemand mit dem Foto helfen?
- Wer ist im Foto am Tisch?
- Wie fahren die vier Freunde zum Flughafen?
- Was ist das Problem auf der Autobahn?
- Was sucht Paul im Flugzeug?
- Wo wollen Paul und Claire nächstes Jahr Urlaub machen?
- Warum?

Quick sentences

Here are five short, useful sentences based on this week's **Story**. Say them quickly in German. Score two points for a fast sentence and one for normal speed.

- Who is it?
- What are we doing/going to do?
- Can you help me, please?
- I believe we have a problem.
- A return ticket, please.

Verbs, verbs!

Say these verb phrases in German.

to arrive, I cannot work, we worked, he was, they bought, I don't know, Can you help me?, Can you speak more slowly, please? she went, do you need?, we have said, you saw, I believe that …, I cannot drink, I want to call, we cannot, would you like to have …, How much does it cost?, I am looking for …, I don't have it

The stories of Paul and Claire

On Day 7 of each of the seven weeks of this **Starter kit** the **Story** for the week is given in full. Tell me in German, in one or two sentences, what each Day 7 **Story** is about.

1 Wir gehen Ski fahren
2 Wo ist Elke?
3 Ich möchte ein Auto kaufen
4 Wir fahren nach Österreich
5 Im Restaurant
6 Ich brauche einen Arzt
7 Auf Wiedersehen München – aber wir haben die Fotos!

Score between 10 and 20 points depending on how well you think you spoke.

Now for your final result

✓ Last word check	/20
✓ Tell me, tell me …	/30
✓ Quick sentences	/10
✓ Verbs, verbs!	/20
✓ The stories of Paul and Claire	/20

Total score /100% **Date** _____

Enter your final result on the **Progress chart** and work out your overall score. Then write this and your name on your **Certificate**.

You can now speak Starter kit German!

This is to certify

that

_____

has successfully completed
the seven-week

German

Starter Kit

course with_____ results

Elizabeth Smith

Tutor

Date